"译"无巨细

英汉互译技巧示例

彭萍◎著

中国宇航出版社

·北京·

版权所有　侵权必究

图书在版编目（CIP）数据

"译"无巨细：英汉互译技巧示例 / 彭萍著. -- 北京：中国宇航出版社，2023.2(2024.9重印)

ISBN 978-7-5159-2167-9

Ⅰ. ①译… Ⅱ. ①彭… Ⅲ. ①英语－翻译－研究 Ⅳ. ①H315.9

中国版本图书馆CIP数据核字(2022)第238009号

策划编辑	冯佳佳	封面设计	李彦生
责任编辑	冯佳佳	责任校对	刘　杰

出版发行	中国宇航出版社		
社　址	北京市阜成路8号	邮　编	100830
	(010) 68768548		
网　址	www.caphbook.com		
经　销	新华书店		
发行部	(010) 68767386		(010) 68371900
	(010) 68767382		(010) 88100613（传真）
零售店	读者服务部		
	(010) 68371105		
承　印	三河市君旺印务有限公司		
版　次	2023年2月第1版		2024年9月第4次印刷
规　格	710×1000	开　本	1/16
印　张	12.25	字　数	200千字
书　号	ISBN 978-7-5159-2167-9		
定　价	39.80元		

本书如有印装质量问题，可与发行部联系调换

前　言

再过两年，我从教就30年了，今年也是我在北外从事翻译教学整整二十年。蓦然回首，一切如白驹过隙，但二十多年来，学翻译、教翻译、研究翻译、做翻译给我的生活带来了无限的满足感和成就感，所以我经常由衷地感慨：幸亏当年考研的时候选择了翻译。实际上，报考研究生时，我毅然决然地选择翻译专业，就是因为自己从学英语开始就怀有一颗初心：做一名翻译家。这么多年过去了，我虽然依然在成为翻译家的路上，但是"翻译"和translation已经成为我近二十多年来使用最多的词。

翻译是一门技艺，也就是说，既是一门技术，又是一门艺术。翻译工作者更是一名工匠，一名充满深情地将语言材料加工成艺术作品的工匠。正是基于这种认识，我一直将自己视为一名匠人，一方面在自己做翻译的过程中打磨、精进自己的技艺，还特别注意翻译经验的积累，以便能够在课堂上传授给自己的学生，写进自己编写的教材，去帮助更多有志于成为翻译工匠的人，或者借助翻译去探索更广阔世界的人。因此，在平时的教学、阅读和翻译实践中，我注重去归纳总结翻译的规律，尤其是翻译实践中非常注重收集体现这些规律的例子，以便课堂上能够举一反三，以便教材中所用例证丰富，同时做到所用素材能够与时俱进。

我自己编写的《实用商务翻译（英汉双向）》和主编的《实用语篇翻译（英汉双向）》在中国宇航出版社出版后，受到读者的青睐，特别是《实用语篇翻译（英汉双向）》，成为很多报考翻译硕士的莘莘学子必读的一本书，很多考研成功"上岸"的同学会在自己的经验中提到这本书，还有很多考上的同学见到我都会提到这本书，这让我感到无比欣慰。有一天，中国宇航出版社的编辑冯佳佳女士找到我，对我说："彭老师，您能不能再编写一本浅显易懂的翻译技巧书？将您认为重要的技巧写出来。"我欣然答应。忙忙碌碌中过去了一些日子，有一天，忽然接到佳佳编辑的微信，请我写出本书的提纲和一个样章，我才意识到这件事真的要提到议程上来，无论多忙，也要尽快写出来。于是，当天晚饭后，我在电脑前开始思考目前我最想和翻译学习者分享哪些翻译技巧，于是一气呵成，"洋洋洒洒"写出了二十条。写完提纲的时候，忽然想起，这本书应该叫"'译'无巨细：英汉互译技巧示例"。"'译'无巨细"是我经常提醒学生的一句话，翻译成英文就是 You can never be too careful in translating，也就是说，"翻译过程中再细心都不为过"。就像我前面说过的，翻译是一门技艺，需要打磨，需要精进，需要细心、细致和严谨的态度。这些技巧讲解中有英译中，也有中译英，其中使用的例子大多都是我平时积累的。因为主要讲解技巧，所以只能用句子做例子。好在翻译的基本操作单位就是句子，句子译好了，就完成了80%，然后再注意中英文各自句与句之间的衔接，篇章也就出来了，这些技巧在一些章节也会提及。书中的例子来自不同文本，更来自不同文体。由此可以看出，无论何种文本，无论何种文体，很多技巧是相通的，因为很多时候，这些技巧处理的是两种语言之间的差异。所以在讲述过程中，我会提到中英文的区别。总之，翻译学习者要将两种语言真正吃透，要了解中英文表象上的差异及其背后隐藏的中西思维差异，这样才能真正"游走于"两种语言之间，轻松进行语言转换，做一位技艺娴熟的翻译匠人。

  这些技巧讲解中，有些技巧我也在自己编写或主编的其他教材里提到过，有些是第一次讲解，但大多数例子都比较新，通俗易懂，希望能够给读者带来灵感。当然，还有些我平时上课总结的技巧由于涉及的点太细没法讲出来，也让我感到遗憾，因为就我本人而言，恨不得把自己知道的全部呈现给读者，从而给更多学习翻译的人以启发和帮助。

  本书在编写过程中参考了众多文章和教材，尽量列在参考书目中，若有遗漏，敬请谅解。感谢中国宇航出版社冯佳佳编辑在本书编辑过程中付出的努力，感谢我的先生刘辛提供的一切支持，感谢我的2022级研究生高羽、李梦姣、缪雨倩、彭格格、涂鑫、王仕琦、王仪舒、张廷玉、张铧丹和郑可馨通读了书稿。感谢我所有的学生在我翻译教学中给予我的灵感，感谢广大读者的厚爱。本书讲解中所使用例句的译文和练习中的参考译文均旨在给读者提供参考，因为不同的译者翻译同一个句子，其译文一定会存在一定的差异，只要原文意思和语气传达准确，只要译文符合目的语的表达习惯，都是正确的。练习参考译文后面的简析旨在为翻译学习者提供一定的提示和指导。本书编写时间有限，如有纰漏，敬请广大读者不吝赐教。

彭萍
2022 年冬于平心斋

目 录

第一章	选　词	/001
第二章	英文主谓结构译为中文三种不同句子结构	/014
第三章	中文主述结构的翻译	/024
第四章	中文无主句的翻译	/032
第五章	英文定语从句的翻译	/043
第六章	英文同位语的翻译	/054
第七章	英文形容词变通翻译的几种情况	/063
第八章	英文名词转译为中文的动词或形容词	/071
第九章	中文动词或形容词译为英文名词	/078
第十章	英文被动语态的翻译	/085
第十一章	英文"形容词+名词"和中文"名词+形容词"互换	/096
第十二章	英译中名词的重复和中译英名词的省译	/104
第十三章	中文连动式的翻译	/112
第十四章	中文范畴名词省译和英译中添加范畴名词	/123
第十五章	英译中修辞增译和中译英修辞省译	/130
第十六章	英文的替代和中文的重复	/141
第十七章	中文重复名词和动词的翻译	/149
第十八章	英文长句的翻译	/156
第十九章	中文长句的翻译	/167
第二十章	英译中的合句处理	/177
主要参考文献		/185

第一章 选 词

英语学习者往往通过英文单词的中文意思记忆单词，这样做的后果就是，翻译时往往将英文单词和中文意思一一对应起来，造成用词不当。实际上，几乎每一种语言都有一词多义的现象。具体来说，英文单词和中文词语并非一一对应的关系，往往一个英文单词对应几个中文意思。因此，翻译过程中要根据词语所在的语境确定其在上下文中的具体含义。另外，词在上下文中的意义广狭、感情色彩、语体色彩等都应根据语境进行判断，然后在目的语中选择恰当的对应词。

一、根据词在语境中的含义选词

词的实际意思取决于所在的语境。比如，英文中 idea 一词在中文中的对应表达就不止一个，如"思想""想法""观点""观念""主意""计划""打算"等，翻译时要根据具体的语境选择其中的一个。可以看以下几个例子。

◇ 例 1

I can't understand his strange *ideas* at all.
我对他那些奇怪的<u>想法</u>一点都不理解。

◇ 例 2

What is your *idea* of what is going on?
你对正在发生的一切有什么<u>看法</u>？

◇ 例 3

It's my *idea* to hold the party outside the house.
在房子外面举办派对是我的<u>主意</u>。

◇ 例 4

This book gives you some *idea* of life in ancient Greece.
这本书可以使你了解古希腊人的生活。

◇ 例 5

Suddenly an *idea* flashed across me.
突然，我脑中闪过一个念头。

由此可见，一个英文单词及其中文翻译不是一对一的映射关系。有时，相同的词在同一句话中意思也不尽相同，需要选择不同的中文词才能传达原文的意思。例如：

◇ 例 6

Needing some *light* to see by, the burglar crossed the room with a *light* step to *light* the *light* with the *light* green shade.
夜贼需要一点亮光来看东西，便蹑手蹑脚穿过房间，点亮了那盏带浅绿色灯罩的灯。

汉英翻译更是如此，切记不可望"词"生"译"。

◇ 例 7

这不仅是简单恢复一个入学考试，而是一个国家和时代的拐点，许多人的命运从此彻底发生改变。
It was more than a resumption of an examination, but a turning point for the whole country and the beginning of a new age, since so many Chinese people's *life* was completely changed after that year.

◇ 例 8

党的十八大以来，我们提出践行正确义利观，推动构建以合作共赢为核心的新型国际关系、打造人类命运共同体，打造遍布全球的伙伴关系网络。

Since the 18th CPC National Congress, we have advocated the principle of upholding the greater good and pursuing shared interests, and facilitated the building of a new model of international relations featuring cooperation and mutual benefit, a community of shared *future* for humankind, and a partnership network that links all parts of the world.

◇ 例 9

外商投资企业在提升中国经济增长质量和效益的同时，分享中国经济发展红利。

Foreign-funded companies have shared the *benefits* of China's economic development, while helping improve the quality and *performance* of the economy.

这里的"效益"不能译成 profit，"红利"不能译成 bonus，根据上下文意思分别译成 performance 和 benefits。

二、根据语境中词义的广狭选词

英文和中文词汇在不同上下文中都有广狭意义之分。例如，英文中的 cat 有时译成"猫"（狭义），有时译成"猫科动物"（广义），cousin 有时译成"表亲"这一广义概念，有时译成"表哥"或"表姐"等狭义概念。中文的"农业"如果表示广义概念，就要译成 agriculture，表示狭义概念时则译为 farming。再看下面的例子。

◇ 例 10

The *man* who, in old age, can see his life in this way, will not suffer from the fear of death.（广义）

一个人年老的时候，如果能这样看待生命，就不会经受恐惧死亡的痛苦。

◇ 例 11

She was more of a *man* than any of them.（狭义）
她比他们中间的任何一个人都更像男子汉。

例 10 中的 man 实际上泛指人，属于广义概念，根据上下文译为"人"；例 11 中的 man 则指男性，是狭义概念，根据上下文译为"男子汉"。

◇ **例 12**

语言是在实践的过程中逐渐形成的。（广义）

Language has been formed gradually during practice.

◇ **例 13**

苏州是吴文化的发源地，苏绣、绘画、篆刻、昆曲、评弹、苏剧以及饮食、服饰、语言等融汇成其丰富内涵。（狭义）

Suzhou is the cradle of Wu Culture, which covers Suzhou Embroidery, painting, seal cutting, Kunqu Opera, Suzhou Ballad Singing, and Suzhou Opera as well as the local cuisine, costume and *dialect*.

以上两个例子中，例 12 中的"语言"为泛指，是广义词，例 13 中的"语言"则是狭义词，表示苏州地方的语言，实指"方言"。因此，两个例子中的"语言"在英文中翻译成了不同的词。

三、根据语境中词的感情色彩选词

英文和中文的词都会带有自己的感情色彩，有的表示肯定和赞许，带有喜悦之情；有的则表示否定和贬斥，带有憎恶之感。当然，也有一些词是中性词，没有褒贬之分。例如，中文的"成果""结果""后果"三个词，"成果"就是褒义词，"后果"就是贬义词，"结果"则是中性词。英文中，描述一个人很节俭往往用 thrifty，描述一个人很吝啬往往使用 stingy，这两个词就有褒贬之分，前者是褒义词，后者是贬义词；而中文的"节俭"与"吝啬"本来就体现了褒贬之分。翻译时，要根据词在上下文中的感情色彩在目的语中选择对应的词汇。翻译过程中，译者一定要注意根据语境忠实地传达出原文的感情色彩。比如，delicate upbringing 应译成"娇生惯养"，显然属于贬义；delicate touch 指写作中注重细节，属于褒义，可以译成"生花妙笔"。再看下面几个例子。

◇ 例 14

Alfred was intensely *ambitious*, obsessed with the idea of becoming rich.（贬义）
阿尔弗雷德过于<u>野心勃勃</u>，一心想着发财。

◇ 例 15

Although he is very young, he is very *ambitious* in his research work.（褒义）
虽然他很年轻，但是在研究工作中很有<u>雄心壮志</u>。

以上两个例子中的 ambitious 显然感情色彩不同，所以译文中选择了不同的中文词，以区分感情色彩。

◇ 例 16

他们这件事做得很<u>漂亮</u>，值得赞扬。（褒义）
They have done it quite *well* and deserve praises.

◇ 例 17

他尽说<u>漂亮</u>话。（贬义）
He is good at *high-flown* talks.

这两个例子中，例 16 的"漂亮"是褒义词，译文使用了 well，例 17 中的"漂亮"显然是贬义词，所以根据感情色彩以及后面的搭配译成了 high-flown。

再比如，中文的"欲望"如果用作褒义词时，英语可以译成 desire 或 longing；如果表达"欲壑难填"时，"欲望"一词就需要使用英语中带贬义色彩的词，如 avarice 或者 greed，即 Avarice knows no bound 或者 Greed knows no bound。

四、根据语境中词义的语体色彩选词

中英文的文体有正式和非正式之分，有古典与现代之分，有文学性和非文学性之分，有口语和书面语之分。语体色彩对翻译中的选词也会产生影响。不妨看看下面的例子。

◇ 例 18

It was too early for a *heavy fall of leaves* in the year, but nevertheless, the garden was *covered*.

还未到一年中<u>落叶纷飞</u>的时节，花园里却已<u>落叶满地</u>。

◇ 例 19

It is the thing he cannot bear to lose, it is the thing whose *passing* he watches with infinite sorrow and regret, it is the thing whose loss he must *lament forever*, and it is the thing whose loss he really welcomes *with a sad and secret joy*, *the thing* he would never willingly relive again, could it be restored to him by any magic.

谁都想让青春永驻，眼睁睁地看着青春<u>流逝</u>，心中都会涌起无数的忧伤和追悔，都会充满<u>难以排遣</u>的<u>哀怨</u>，都会<u>悲喜交集</u>。即便有奇迹出现，令青春回头，谁也不会再去重温那<u>蹉跎岁月</u>。

例 18 和例 19 出自散文，翻译时要注意贴近散文的风格，选词要贴近其语体色彩，译文中的"落叶纷飞""落叶满地""流逝""难以排遣""哀怨""悲喜交集"和"蹉跎岁月"等词汇符合中文读者的审美情趣，所以从选词上讲，以上两个译文是成功的。

◇ 例 20

叶下的洁白如玉雕的荷花，到过午后，像慢慢地将花朵闭起。偶然一两只蜜蜂飞来飞去，还留恋着花香的气味，<u>不肯即行归去</u>。红霞照在湛绿的水上，<u>散为金光</u>。

The flowers under the leaves, *as pure as white jade carvings*, seemed to close up their petals after noon. Occasionally, a couple of bees would hover around, *lured* by the scent, *reluctant to* depart. The *turquoise* water *shimmered* with the *crimson rays* of the setting sun *dancing* on it.

◇ 例 21

该书也是一部实录性质的历史著作，真实地记录了明末农业、手工业、商业、宗教等方面的现实，犹如一幅明末风俗画的<u>长卷</u>，从东到西，展现了从江南水乡到西南边疆生活的<u>千姿万态</u>，<u>形象生动</u>，<u>绚丽多彩</u>。

It is also a historical book recording agriculture, handicraft, commerce and religion in the late Ming Dynasty. Like a *vivid* genre painting, it depicts the *lifestyles of different regions*, from the lower reaches of the Changjiang River to the southwestern frontier of China.

例 20 和例 21 是中文散文，下划线部分描写色彩浓郁，翻译成英文时在传达原文信息的同时，尽量在英文中选择一些比较符合散文文体的词汇。当然，由于两种语言背后的思维模式不同，中文里有些描写性的词汇无法译成英文，如例 21 的"千姿百态"和"绚丽多彩"。即使是"生动形象"也只需使用一个 vivid。

不仅散文如此，实用文体也是如此，选词要符合语体色彩。请看下面旅游文本和法律文本的例子。

◆ 例 22

The lake plateau *glistens* in the afternoon light; the forests of Swiss pine are *redolent* with the *scent* of fresh resin; and in the villages the Engadin houses and their stunning façades *bask in the sunshine*.

高原湖泊在午后阳光的照射下<u>波光粼粼</u>，瑞士松树林<u>散</u>发着新鲜树脂的<u>芳香</u>，恩嘎丁村里的住宅及其绝美的外墙沐浴在温暖的阳光里。

◆ 例 23

The route *leads* to 22 lakes, to the Rhône and Aletsch glaciers, along *mighty* rivers and to the most *impressive* viewpoints high above *raging* white waters.

该线路<u>途经</u> 22 座湖泊及罗纳河和阿莱奇冰川，沿着壮观的河流蜿蜒伸展。游客还可前往最令人陶醉的观景点，俯瞰脚下咆哮翻滚的白色浪花。

◆ 例 24

这里<u>千峰竞秀</u>，有奇峰 72 座，其中天都峰、莲花峰、光明顶都在海拔 1,800

米以上，<u>拔地擎天</u>，<u>气势磅礴</u>，<u>雄姿灵秀</u>。

Here you can enjoy 72 *magnificent* peaks, with Tiandu, Lianhua and Guangmingding above 1,800 meters in altitude. They form into *spectacular* scenery.

◆ 例 25

<u>城内外遍布名胜古迹</u>。寒山寺，<u>诗韵钟声</u>，<u>脍炙人口</u>；虎丘，千年古塔，<u>巍然屹立</u>；天平山，<u>奇石嶙峋</u>，<u>枫林如锦</u>；洞庭东山，<u>湖光山色</u>，<u>花果连绵</u>。

The city *abounds with scenic spots*. The popular Hanshan Temple, with its *charming* bell, has inspired many a *poetic mind*. On the Tiger Hill stands a thousand-year-old pagoda in *majesty*. The Tianping Hill is featured by *rock formations and maple woods* while *luxurian*t *fruit-trees* add to the beauty of East Dongting Hill and *the lakes around*.

以上四个例子均来自旅游文本，原文均注重描写所介绍景点的美丽，所以选词也要符合该文体的特点，无论是中译文还是英译文都注意到了这一点。但是，前文提过，由于中英文背后的思维模式不同，中译英时，译文显得比原文简单一些，才是真正的翻译。翻译学习者和翻译工作者必须认识到这一点，否则，译出的英文会显得冗余累赘。

◆ 例 26

This Contact and any rights or obligations *hereunder* are *not transferable or assignable* by one party to this Contract without the *consent* of the other party *hereto*.

未经另一方<u>许可</u>，合同一方<u>不得转让</u>本合同及本合同规定的权利和义务。

◆ 例 27

This Agreement does not *constitute* the *conveyance* of ownership with respect to or a license to any Confidential Information.

本协议不<u>构</u>成对任何保密信息所有权或许可的<u>转让</u>。

以上两个例子中，原文斜体部分用词都比较正式，而且符合英语合同的用词特点，特别是 hereunder、hereto 等古体词，一般用于法律文本。另外，英文合同中还倾向使用名词，如例 26 中的 consent 和例 27 中的 conveyance 和 respect。当然，这些词译成中文时无法一一对应，但是中文合同选词也非常正式。

◇ 例 28

本协议终止后，双方应根据就信息返还或销毁达成的协议，于协议终止后 30 日内向对方返还或销毁所有资料的书面文件和电子文件。

Upon *termination* of this Agreement, both parties *shall*, *in accordance with* the agreement on information return or destruction, return to the other party or destroy all the written work excluded from that covered by their agreement within 30 days *thereafter*.

例 28 原文也写得非常正式，特别是下划线部分，显示出中文合同的文体特点。译成英文时，根据语气选择使用情态动词 shall、名词 termination 和 accordance 以及古体词 thereafter，传达出原文的语体风格。

◇ 例 29

We should be *obliged* if you would give us a quotation per metric ton CFR Lagos, Nigeria.

敬请报给我方每公吨尼日利亚拉格斯成本加运费价。

◇ 例 30

承蒙贵方 6 月 15 日来函，提出我方可以作为代理处，代办贵公司办公家具，谨致谢意。

We are *obliged* for your letter of 15th June, in which you offer us the agency for your office furniture.

例 29 和例 30 属于商务文书，例 29 中 obliged 是英语商务文书中的常用词汇，中译文使用了商务文书常用词汇"敬请"；例 30 原文下划线部分也是中文商务文书常用词汇，尤其是下划线部分体现了语体色彩，翻译时使用了 obliged。

五、根据语境中词的文化意义选词

语言是文化的载体。由于各民族地理、历史背景不同，文化差异也就十分显著，这种差异可导致对词的联想意义不同。翻译过程中要考虑到语言的文化语境。一般说来，带有文化特色的词要根据上下文采取适当的翻译策略，以读者明白其中的意思为准。

◇ 例 31

My brother is the *black sheep* of the family.
我弟弟是我们家的<u>害群之马</u>。

◇ 例 32

Kissinger felt that the massive bombing would strengthen the president's *hand* in China.
基辛格觉得这场大规模的轰炸会使总统在中国的<u>腰杆子</u>硬一些。

例 31 和例 32 中的 black sheep 和 hand 有一定的文化含义，如果异化翻译为"黑羊"和"手"，中文读者就很难理解，所以分别归化为"害群之马"和"腰杆子"，中文的这两个比喻比较恰当地传达了原文的意思。

◇ 例 33

鸿渐忽然明白，这姓赵的对自己无礼，是在<u>吃醋</u>，当自己是他的情敌。（《围城》）
It suddenly dawned on Hung-chien that Chao's rudeness toward him had stemmed from *jealousy*, for Chao had obviously taken him as his love rival.（Kelly & Mao 译）

◇ 例 34

高松年神色不动，准是成算在胸，自己冒失寻衅，万一下不来台，反给他笑，闹了出去，人家总说姓方的<u>饭碗打破</u>，老羞成怒。（《围城》）

Since Kao Sung-nien never changed his expression, Kao must have a plan already worked out. If he risked going into start of a quarrel and found himself out on a limb, he'd just be laughed. If the story got out, people would say that when Fang *lost his job*, his shame turned into resentment.（Kelly & Mao 译）

以上两个例子的下划线部分同样不能进行字面翻译，不能"保持异国情调"，而是根据英文的表达习惯进行翻译，将"吃醋"和"饭碗打破"分别译成了 jealousy 和 lose one's job。

总之，翻译时，要根据词的含义、感情色彩、词义广狭、语体和文体色彩以及文化语境进行选词，不仅要仔细考虑、用心斟酌，还要善于使用词典，力求在译文中找到相对应的词语，以保证意思和风格的忠实以及译文的流畅。

拓展练习

翻译下列句子，请注意选词。

1. When it is *tough*, do it *tough*.
2. The fog *brooded* over the village by the lake, where he had been sitting and *brooding* for hours.
3. He was a man of *history*, so you have to be alert.
4. If each of us hires people who are *smaller* than we are, we shall become a company of *dwarfs*. But if each of us hires people who are *bigger* than we are, Ogilvy & Mather will become a company of *giants*.
5. The leaves were washed to the sides of the roads, and lay heaped up over the road-gratings, *masses* of *gorgeous harmonies* in red, brown, and yellow.
6. 奥运会代表和平与荣誉，代表超越自我、团队合作、公平竞争、尊重规则、尊重对手的运动家精神，这些人类文明最精华的特质也将是让我们继续走向共同未来的基础。
7. 可能因一时疏忽，支票还未签名，现寄还贵方，烦请补签。
8. 古人认为时逢太平盛世，便有凤凰飞来。凤凰被认为是百鸟中最尊贵者，为鸟中之王（尽管它是虚构的），有"百鸟朝凤"之说。

9. 饮酒不仅是享受美味，更能抒情达意——或恭迎远客，或举杯欢庆，或借酒消愁。白酒早已融入社会人情生活的方方面面，展现出其独特的精神文化价值。

10. 这里古色古香，环境优雅，不仅可以细闻梵净山茶的淡雅幽香，还能品味中南门老街数百年的沧桑历史。

参考译文与简析

1. 迎难而上。／遇到困难，顽强面对。（第一个 tough 意思是"棘手的，难办的"，第二个 tough 意为"顽强地"，一词多义，因此翻译选词不同。）

2. 雾笼罩着湖边的小村庄，而他已经坐在湖边沉思了几个小时。（第一个 brood 意为"笼罩"，第二个 brood 意为"沉思，忧思"，意思不同，中文对应的词也不同。）

3. 他有着不光彩的过去，你要小心。（根据句子含义，history 表示贬义，因此译成"不光彩的过去"。）

4. 如果我们每个人都雇用比自己"矮小"的人，我们就会变成一群"侏儒"；如果我们每个人都雇用比自己"高大"的人，奥美就会成为一家"巨人"公司。（这里的 small、big、dwarf 和 giant 都是比喻，可以直译，但需注意前两个单词分别译成"矮小"和"高大"，而非"小"和"大"。）

5. 落叶被雨水冲到路边，堆积在排水栅格上面，红色的、褐色的、黄色的叶子，一堆堆，一丛丛，既绚丽多彩，又和谐悦目。（英文原文属于描写句，译成中文时要注意保持中文表达的美感，像 mass、gorgeous、harmony 等词的翻译要符合中文读者的审美预期。）

6. The Olympic Games represent peace and honor, the sportsman's spirit of *transcendence*, *teamwork*, *fair play*, and *respect for the rules and the opponents*—the very best qualities of human civilization that will also be the basis for continuing our journey towards *a shared future*. （本句中"超越自我""团队合作""公平竞争""尊重规则""尊重对手"以及"共同未来"要注意选择正确的英语对应词。）

7. Probably through an *oversight*, the check was not signed, and we are returning it to you for your *kind* signature. （该句文体较正式和礼貌，因此译文使用了

oversight 和 kind。)

8. In the ancient times, people believed that the phoenix would appear in *a harmonious era of peace and prosperity* to salute the people, so it has always been regarded as the most worshipped bird and thus the queen of birds (though it only exists in legend) . (应了解"太平盛世"在上下文中的意思，然后再选择适当的单词。另外，整个句子是关于中国文化的，翻译时要注意正确传达含义，使英语读者明白句意和中国文化。)

9. Drinking not only satisfies people's taste, but also helps to *express feelings*. One may drink to *welcome friends from afar*, to *celebrate*, or to *seek solace*. Chinese *baijiu* is an integrated part of *the Chinese people's* life, showing its unique *cultural value*. (该句话原文比较注重描写和抒情，选词要到位，但也要注意英语读者的接受程度，比如"抒情达意""恭迎远客""举杯欢庆""借酒消愁""社会人情""精神文化价值"等，这些词要简化翻译。)

10. With *ancient and elegant ambience*, it is a place where you can not only enjoy the most *fragrant* Mount Fanjing Tea, but also immerse yourself in the *history* of Zhongnanmen Old Town dating back to centuries ago. (原文注重描写，像"古色古香""环境优雅""淡雅幽香""沧桑历史"等词要注意简化翻译。)

第二章　英文主谓结构译为中文三种不同句子结构

一、中英文句子结构的差异

　　词是最小的可以独立运用的意义单位，句子则是语言的基本运用单位，一般情况下，进行篇章翻译时，基本上都以句子为具体的操作单位。尤其是将英文译成汉语时，即使是一个很长的句子，一般也要将整个句子通盘考虑，搞清楚整个句子的逻辑关系，才能将其翻译成既忠实传达原文信息、风格、逻辑关系，又能保持通顺的中文。如果是中译英，有时句子较长，可以根据意群进行切分，然后将切分开的句子逐句译为英文。因此，了解两种语言在句式结构上的异同之处，对翻译来说非常重要。吕叔湘先生曾经说过："英语的语句组织比汉语要严格些；对于它的结构做一番分析，也是学习过程中应有之事。"（2005：182）

　　英文句子的基本结构都是 Subject-Verb（S + V）结构，其中主动语态的主语就是谓语动词所代表动作的发出者，被动语态的主语就是谓语动词所代表动作的承受者。中文句子就不尽如此。譬如，汉语中"中国成功地发射了很多人造卫星"与英语 S+V 结构相似，但不能说完全相同，因为英语句子的主谓之间要保持人称和数的一致，比如 I have read the book、He has read the book 以及 The students have read the book，汉语句子中的动词则不需要根据主语的人称和数进行变化。对这一类句子我们不妨称为"类主谓结构"。但是，上面那句话中文还可以写成"人造卫星，中国已成功发射了很多颗。"这句话从形式上看并不是主谓结构，其中"人造卫星"可以看作一个"话题"，"中国已成功地发射了很多颗"可以看作是对这一话题的"评述"。再比如，"这封信虽然引经据典，却犯了一个严重的错误"中主要结构就是"这封信犯了一个错误"，而实际上"信"无法"犯错误"。

因此，我们不妨将这类句子称为"伪主谓结构"，或者就叫做"话题－评述句"，简称为"主述结构"。中文还有一种句子也是很常见的，即无主句。如"出太阳了"和"吃得苦中苦，方为人上人"等。

中文句子结构比较多样，那么英文主谓结构就不能句句按照原文的主谓结构来翻译，有时不得不进行调整，才符合中文的表达习惯。换言之，英文的主谓结构需要根据情况译成中文中以上三种不同的结构。

二、英文主谓结构译为中文三种不同结构

（一）译成中文的类主谓结构

有些英文句子译成中文时，可以使用中文的类主谓结构，特别是英文主动语态句子的主谓结构，而且谓语动词不是 be 或者 have 及其同义词的句子。不少英语句子都可以这样翻译。

◇ 例 1

Many restaurants and stores in Engelberg offer local specialities.

英格堡的许多餐馆和商店都提供当地特产。

◇ 例 2

What makes Wikipedia interesting is how it gets made: Ordinary people submit entries for different topics and then revise them over time.

维基百科的引人之处在于其编纂过程：普通人提供不同主题的词条，然后不断修正。

◇ 例 3

The organization deals with all matters concerning women, focusing on the elimination of legal discrimination against women and the promotion of real equality between men and women.

该组织处理有关妇女的一切问题，重点在于消除对女性的法律歧视，推动男女间实现真正平等。

◇ 例 4

The Women's Movement has organized demonstrations against the illegal Turkish occupation of the northern part of Cyprus through mass peaceful marches and has contributed to finding channels of communication between the two communities, creating thus a culture of peace on the island.

妇女运动组织已通过群众和平游行举行示威活动，反对土耳其非法占领塞浦路斯北部，为寻求两个群体间的沟通渠道作出了贡献，在岛上营造出和平的氛围。

◇ 例 5

This fund finances local projects that reduce CO_2 emissions while at the same time strengthening local suppliers and businesses, conserving local resources and offering guests and customers high-quality products and experiences.

该基金为减少二氧化碳排放的当地项目提供资金，促进了当地供应商和企业发展，保护了当地资源，并为客户提供了高质量的产品和体验。

（二）译成中文的主述结构（伪主谓结构）

首先，当英文句中谓动词为 be 动词时，译成中文时一般会省译 be 动词，这样的译文就是中文名词 + 形容词，属于"话题 – 评述"结构或伪主谓结构。请看下面的例子。

◇ 例 6

This increased commitment to climate protection is central, especially for the mountain region.

加强气候保护这一义务至关重要，对山区而言尤为重要。

◇ 例 7

Since Amerindians were descended from two fairly small waves of migration from Asia, *their genepool was small.*

由于美洲印第安人是亚洲两次小规模移民的后代，他们的基因库很小。

◇ 例 8

Whether they ooze Mediterranean atmosphere or mediaeval charm, *Switzerland's weekly markets are as varied and unique as Swiss cities themselves.*

瑞士的每周集市有的洋溢着地中海风情，有的充满中世纪魅力，<u>与瑞士城市本身一样多姿多彩，独具特色</u>。

◇ 例 9

Manfred, Prince of Otranto, had one son and one daughter: the latter, *a most beautiful virgin*, *aged eighteen*, *was called Matilda*. Conrad, the son, *was three years younger*, *a homely youth*, *sickly*, and of no promising disposition; yet he was the darling of his father, who never showed any symptoms of affection to Matilda.

曼弗雷德是奥特朗托的公爵。他有两个孩子，<u>女儿叫玛蒂尔达，18 岁，美丽纯洁，待字闺中</u>。儿子叫康拉德，<u>比姐姐小三岁，其貌不扬，病恹恹的</u>，从性格上看，成不了什么大器。尽管如此，父亲还是对他百般疼爱，对他姐姐却漠不关心。

以上例子的译文中，有多处名词 + 形容词这样的"话题 – 评述"结构，也可以视为伪主谓结构。

其次，英文句子的主要结构中谓语动词是 have 或者 have 的同义词，后面的宾语也有形容词修饰，即句子的主要结构是 S+V（have/boast）+Adj.+O 的模式，这类句子译成中文时一般会省译谓语动词，形容词调整到宾语后作为描述性内容，就变成了中文的主述结构，即伪主谓结构。请看下面的例子。

◇ 例 10

Switzerland boasts an astounding 65,000 km of hiking trails—enough to satisfy every nature lover.

<u>瑞士的徒步小径总长度 65,000 公里，令人惊叹</u>，足以满足每一位自然爱好者的需求。

◇ 例 11

Any science may be likened to a river, says a Johns Hopkins biologist, Professor Carl P. Swanson. "*It has its obscure and unpretentious beginning; its quiet stretches as well as its rapids; its periods of drought as well as of fullness.*"

约翰·霍普金斯大学的生物学家卡尔·斯旺森教授指出，任何一门科学都可以比作一条河，"河的源头<u>隐隐约约，并不引人注目</u>；水流<u>时而平缓，时而湍急</u>；有枯水期，也有丰水期。"

◇ 例 12

Tourists have a tendency to pack much more than they really need.

游客携带物品往往比真正需要的多得多。

以上例子中，例 10 和例 11 译文的下划线部分以及例 12 译文整句话的主结构都没有动词，基本是"名词 + 形容词"结构，即主述结构或伪主谓结构，读起来比直译更加通顺，更具描述性，符合中文的表达习惯。

第三，英文中有些句子翻译时需要将时间或地点提到中文译文的最前面，而中文的时间和地点前置时一般不加介词，看上去是"名词 + 动词"结构，但实际上，表示时间或地点的名词与后面的动词并不构成真正的主谓关系，因此这样的译文也是伪主谓结构。

◇ 例 13

In Cyprus there are many women's organizations, trade unions and other non-governmental organizations, active in the promotion of women's rights and equal opportunities.

<u>塞浦路斯</u>有很多妇女组织、工会和其他非政府组织，这些组织积极致力于为女性争取权利和平等机会。

◇ 例 14

Cars are forbidden *in Wengen and Mürren*, two of the most touristy villages.

两座游客最喜欢的村庄翁根和米伦禁止汽车通行。

◇ 例 15

These delicacies feature *in the region's restaurants and "pintes"*.
该地区的餐厅和"pintes（典型的沃州小酒馆）"均供应这些特色美食。

以上三个例子中，原文斜体部分均为介词短语作状语，译成中文时这些地点状语提到句首，按照中文的表达习惯省略介词，变成了表面看去是"名词+动词"的中文结构，实际上属于主述结构或伪主谓结构。

当然还有一些英文句子译成中文时需要根据中文的表达习惯进行调整，结果也成了主述结构或伪主谓结构。请看下面的例子。

◇ 例 16

Sustainability starts on a small scale, with each individual.
可持续发展从小事做起，从我做起。

◇ 例 17

Switzerland is one of the world's leading countries when it comes to recycling and waste management, with almost 90% of PET bottles being put to new use.
回收利用和废物管理方面，瑞士在国际上一直遥遥领先，几乎 90% 的聚酯瓶子都实现了回收使用。

（三）译成中文的无主句

中文有一类句子是由动宾词组或其他动词性词组构成，可以称之为无主句。这些无主句有的表示"存在"和"出现"，例如"出太阳了""跑出一条狗"等；有的表示一种客观现象，如"下雨了"；有的表示客观公正，如"禁止携带宠物进入公园"；有的表示科学道理或客观存在，如"在页岩丰富的地方可以发现石油"；有的是谚语，如"不到黄河心不死""不入虎穴，焉得虎子"等。因此，英文的一些句子，特别是表示上述内容的句子，翻译时应该考虑省略主语，译成中文的无主句。

首先，在一些旅游、科普等英文材料中，如果句子的主语是第二人称 you，这个 you 实际上是一种泛指主语，并不指代具体某一个人，这时首先考虑省译 you，译成中文的无主句。请看下面的例子。

◇ 例 18

You can buy any number of fresh, high-quality products from the surrounding Bernese countryside.

可以购买伯尔尼附近乡村出产的各种新鲜优质产品。

◇ 例 19

You stay in the hotel of your choice but as part of a half-board arrangement, you have the daily option of savouring creative cuisine at one of 20 other hotels or restaurants.

入住自己选择的酒店，但作为半食宿安排的一部分，可以每天选择在其他 20 家宾馆或餐馆享用创意美食。

◇ 例 20

When you build a dam, you will destroy the eco-system downstream.
建造大坝就会破坏下游的生态环境。

个别情况下，英文句子也会使用 we 作为泛指的主语，并没有实指，而是虚指大家，这时也应首先考虑省译 we，变成中文的无主句。

◇ 例 21

Nature is our capital—if we are to preserve it, we must treat it with awe and respect.

大自然是人类的资本——要保护大自然，就必须以敬畏和尊重的态度对待大自然。

英文中一些被动语态的句子可以翻译成中文的无主句，特别是有情态动词的被动语态。

◇ 例 22

Thanks to a special steam extraction system, the typical steam plume can be prevented.

由于使用了特殊的蒸汽抽取系统，可以防止产生典型的蒸汽羽流。

◇ 例 23

Governments of low-income countries must be persuaded to give greater priority to education in their discussions with donors, and to allocate to it a greater share of the savings from debt relief.

必须说服低收入国家政府在与捐助国商谈时进一步优先考虑教育部门，同时将更多债务减免额分配给教育部门。

这两句话的主结构都是情态动词后面加被动语态，译成了中文的无主句。当然也有其他被动语态的句子可以译成中文的无主句，特别是一些科普材料中的被动语态以及表示建议等的被动语态。请看下面的例子。

◇ 例 24

Additional International Standards may be added to the series in the future.

将来有可能对本系列标准增加若干项国际标准。

◇ 例 25

It is recommended that you make a reservation as soon as possible.

建议尽早预订。

◇ 例 26

At the organizational level, a sustainability group has been formed, consisting of an employee from each sector, the director and a sustainability manager.

在组织层面，成立了一个可持续发展小组，由部门的一名员工、主管和一名可持续发展经理组成。

　　以上几个例子的原文都是被动语态，句子中其他地方也没有出现动作的发出者，根据具体语境和中文的表达习惯译成了无主句。

拓展练习

翻译下列句子，请注意英文句式在中译文中的变化。

1. With the project "Davos Climate 2030" and the creation of the "myclimate Climate Fund Davos", the world-famous holiday, leisure and congress resort Davos is taking a big step towards sustainable tourism.
2. The destination organisation, numerous companies and the municipality have been committed to sustainability for years.
3. *It* now takes many, very small and many big steps to make the goal come true.
4. In order to pursue a sustainable strategy, *the idea was born*: *turbines should be added* to the existing infrastructure in order to produce ecological electricity from hydropower.
5. With the Davos Klosters Golf Card, *you* benefit from reduced green fees on our courses and play either 10×9 holes or 5×18 holes.
6. If *you* really want to get into the Bernese atmosphere, *you* should really think about paying the market a visit.
7. If *you* still prefer to be completely independent, then rent a low-emission electric car.
8. Once *you* have your own travel cutlery set, *you*'ll never want to be without it.
9. Black's theory was that what did in the American Indians was their own lack of biodiversity.
10. Almost always the remains of shells, and other proofs of sea life, are found *close to the oil*.

参考译文与简析

1. 随着"2030达沃斯气候"项目的开展和"达沃斯气候基金"的创建,世界著名度假、休闲胜地和会议中心达沃斯正朝着可持续旅游迈出一大步。(译成了中文的主述结构,即伪主谓结构。)

2. 目的地组织、众多公司和市政府多年来一直致力于可持续发展。(原文的结构基本没有变化。)

3. 如今需要很多细微而又巨大的努力才能实现目标。(该句无须译出主语,译成中文的无主句更通顺。)

4. 为追求可持续战略,<u>产生了一个创意</u>:在现有基础设施中<u>添加涡轮机</u>,以便利用水力发电产生生态电力。(该句原文前后两部分都是被动语态,但如果直译则不符合中文的表达习惯。译文变被动为主动,并使用了中文无主句。)

5. 使用达沃斯-克洛斯特斯高尔夫会员卡,可以在我们的球场享受果岭费减免优惠,并且可以打10×9洞或5×18洞。(原文的you属于泛指主语,应省略不译,整句话译成了无主句。)

6. 如果真的想融入伯尔尼的氛围,就应该认真考虑去集市逛一逛。(原文主语也是you,属于泛指主语,可以省译,整句话译成中文无主句。)

7. 如果仍喜欢完全独立旅行,可以租一辆低排放的电动汽车。(原文主句是祈使句,从句是you作主语,you省译,整句译文是无主句。)

8. 一旦拥有自己的旅行餐具套装,会永远离不开它。(原文的you属于泛指主语,应省略不译,整句话译成无主句。)

9. 布莱克的理论认为,发生在美洲印第安人身上的一切是因为他们缺乏生物多样性。(根据中文的表达习惯,译文后半部分变成了主述结构,即伪主谓结构。)

10. <u>石油的附近</u>几乎总会发现贝壳的遗骸和其他海生生物的遗迹。(原文的地点close to the oil译成了名词短语"石油的附近",这样译文就变为主述结构,即伪主谓结构。)

第三章　中文主述结构的翻译

在第二章中讲到，中文的句式结构和英文句式结构存在一定差异。中文除与英文主谓结构相似的主谓结构（类主谓结构）外，还有很多句子看似是主谓结构，其实并不是，这一类句子我们称之为主述结构（"主题–评述"结构）。这类句子很容易译为中式英语，即大家所谓的 Chinglish。那么，怎样避免出现这些问题呢？首先，要认识到，这类句子不是和英文主谓结构类似的句子；其次，按照英文的思维模式找到真正的主谓搭配，也就是先在中文语内用贴近英文的主谓结构解释一遍。比如，"我们的工作取得了巨大成绩"可以在语内解释为"我们在工作中取得了巨大成绩"这样的类主谓结构，然后再翻译就简单多了（We have achieved so much in our work.）。再比如，"这封信犯了一个严重的错误"，实际上按照真正的主谓结构解释，应该是"(某人)在这封信中犯了一个严重的错误"(She/He made a serious mistake in the letter.) 或者"一个严重的错误被犯了"(A serious mistake was made in the letter.)，然后再翻译成英语。下面具体讲一下中文主述结构的翻译。

一、"名词 + 形容词"主述结构的翻译

中文的一些主述结构是"名词 + 形容词"结构，这类句子一般译成英文的"名词 +be 动词 + 形容词 + 名词"结构。

◆ 例 1

他虽已是年近五旬，但依然一表人才。

Though in his late forties, he was still a handsome man.

◇ 例 2

新来的英语老师和蔼可亲，平易近人。

The new English teacher is an amiable lady.

◇ 例 3

这项计划完美无缺。

It is a perfect plan.

◇ 例 4

太湖奇峰环抱，烟水迷蒙，自然天成的湖光山色，美不胜收。

The Taihu Lake, surrounded by hills and veiled in mist, is a magnificent natural landscape.

◇ 例 5

长城脚下最美雪乡，场面恢宏，造型大气，景致优美。

Located in the most beautiful snow land at the foot of the Great Wall, it is a magnificent park.

有些中文句子是"名词＋名词＋形容词"这样的主述结构，这类句子译成英文时一般转译为"主语 +have（或者 have 的同义词）+宾语"的主谓结构。请看下面的例子。

◇ 例 6

小镇景色十分迷人，气候也十分温和。

The town has stunning scenery and a mild climate.

◇ 例 7

安徽地处暖温带与亚热带过渡地区，气候温暖湿润，四季分明。

Anhui, located in a transitional zone between warm temperate and subtropical zones, has a warm and humid climate with four distinct seasons.

◇ 例 8

居庸关长城历史悠久、风光秀美,两旁山峦重叠、山势雄奇。

The Juyongguan Great Wall, with a long history, has magnificent mountains on both sides and marvelous scenery around.

二、伪主谓结构"名词+动词"主述句的翻译

中文有一些句子是"名词+动词"的结构,看上去与英文的主谓结构相似,但实际上这个名词与后面的动词不构成真正意义上的主谓关系。这种句子结构与英文主谓结构相比,就可以算作伪主谓结构,也是主述结构的一种。此类句子如果按照表面结构进行翻译,很容易译为中式英文,所以要十分小心,翻译时需要找到能够发出动词动作的真正主语,如果找不到,则使用被动语态。请看下面的例子。

◇ 例 9

雪场采用人工造雪,保证了雪量的充足和雪质完美。

The manmade snow in the park ensures snow quantity and quality.

这个句子乍看上去"雪场"是主语,"采用"和"保证"是谓语,但细读会发现"雪场"不能发出"采用"和"保证"的动作,这里的"雪场"实际上是地点状语,因此,不能直接翻译为表面的"主谓"结构,而应分析句子,将"人工造雪"作主语,"保证"作谓语。

◇ 例 10

"一带一路"建设已经迈出坚实步伐。

A solid first step has been taken in the implementation of the Belt and Road Initiative.

例 10 的原文乍一看,"建设"好像是主语,"迈出"好像是谓语,但实际上前者并不能发出后面的动作,是一种伪主谓结构。"迈出步伐"的主语应该是人,

但这里没有提及，所以翻译成了被动语态。

◇ 例 11

截至 2017 年年底，中国海淘用户已达到 6,500 万人，预计 2025 年该数据将达到 3 亿人。

By the end of 2017, the number of overseas shopping platform users in China had amounted to 65 million, and it is expected to rise to 300 million in 2025.

例 11 的原文从表面来看，"用户"是主语，"达到"是谓语，实际上两者并不构成主谓关系，译文不能是"the users... reach..."这种中式英文结构，分析后会发现，英文中真正的主语应该是用户的人数，因此将 number 作主语，谓语动词可以使用 reach 或者 amount to。下面的例 12 也是如此，前面三个名词与后面"流传着传说"并不构成实际上的主谓关系，不能按照顺序翻译，只能解读为"关于……有着美丽的传说"。

◇ 例 12

布达拉宫、冈仁波齐山、纳木错圣湖等都流传着极为美丽的传说。

There are fascinating legends about the Potala Palace, the Kangrinboqe Mountain and the Namtso Lake.

三、其他主述结构的翻译

中文的主述结构有很多表现形式，有些没有太多规律可循，但是译者在翻译这类句子时需要认真阅读，要敏锐地发现有些句子是主述结构，然后根据英文主谓结构的特点进行翻译。请看下面的例子。

◇ 例 13

与平昌冬奥会时相比，我们此刻身处一个看上去挑战更严峻的时刻。

At this moment, we are faced with more severe challenges than at the PyeongChang Winter Olympics.

例 13 中"我们身处一个挑战更严峻的时刻"不是真正的主谓结构，应该解读为"我们面临更严峻的挑战"，这样再译成英语就容易多了。

✧ 例 14

中华民族的明天，可以说是"长风破浪会有时"。

The Chinese nation will have a better future though it will have to brave strong winds and waves.

例 14 原文的主结构是"明天"和"长风破浪会有时"，因此，也不是英语意义上的主谓结构，翻译时要仔细分析，可以解读出"中华民族会有一个更好的明天"，"长风破浪"是指中华民族会经历一些风浪，可以作为让步状语。

✧ 例 15

2008 年北京奥运会开幕式更多是向世界展示中国，而到了 2022 年，则是更多地去阐述人类共通的情感，是从"我"转向"我们"。

The opening ceremony of the 2008 Beijing Olympics was more about presenting China to the world, and in 2022 it is more about the common feelings of human beings, shifting from "me" to "us".

例 15 中"北京奥运会开幕式是……更是……"实际上和后面也不构成主谓关系，翻译时需要分析解读，找到符合英语逻辑的表达结构。

✧ 例 16

尊诗圣的是因为需要诗圣，做诗圣的只能贫苦潦倒。

People honoured Du Fu as the Poetry Sage out of their need while the poet himself lived in poverty and frustration.

例 16 原文的两个小分句实际上都是中文的主述结构，不是严格意义上的主谓结构，因此需要译者认真分析。分析后会发现，第一个小分句的主语应该是"人们"，谓语动词应该是"尊……为诗圣"，第二个小分句的主语是"诗圣本人"，谓语动词应该是"生活"或者"过着……的生活"。

◇ 例 17

一个文人，身后能达到如此的豪华气派，地球上怕再也没有第二个人了。

There has probably been no other scholar like Confucius, who has been so magnificently honoured since his death.

例 17 中"一个文人"是话题，后面都是评述性内容。"身后能达到如此的豪华气派"也属于"话题 – 评述"结构。这里的"一个文人"指孔子，分析后会发现可以这样理解："再也没有第二个像孔子这样的文人了"，"身后达到豪华气派"是修饰孔子的，意思是"得到了如此高度的尊重 / 尊敬"。

◇ 例 18

中国减贫实践表明，治国之道，富民为始；民之贫富，国之责任。

China's success in poverty alleviation has proven that governance of a country starts with the needs of the people, and that their prosperity is the responsibility of the government.

例 18 中"治国之道，富民为始；民之贫富，国之责任"也是主述结构，需要翻译时解读为英语的主谓结构。

从对以上例子的分析可以看出，翻译中文主述结构时，首先要认识到句子不是主谓结构；其次是根据英文的主谓关系先在中文进行语内解读，分析哪个词在英译文中可以作主语，哪个动词可以作这个主语的谓语动词。换言之，如果要翻译得地道，先要在语内进行翻译。因此，要想翻译好中文的主述结构，做好语内翻译是第一步。

拓展练习

翻译下列句子，请注意中文句式在英译文中的变化。

1. 数百万原来享受公费医疗的城市居民，今后的医疗费用要自己承担一部分。
2. 王烈器度宽宏，学业精深，年轻时名望在管宁、邴原之上。
3. 杭州等13个跨境电子商务综合试验区积极探索建立以"六体系两平台"为核心的管理制度，形成了12个方面成熟经验做法，面向全国复制推广。
4. 云蒙山是北京著名的国家森林公园，山势耸拔，奇峰异石多姿，飞瀑流泉遍布，林木花草馥郁，自然风景十分优美。
5. 世界好，中国才能好；中国好，世界才更好。
6. 农村及偏远地区信息化应用水平进一步提升。
7. 大运河的无锡段又窄又深，两岸是一排排青瓦白墙的老式民居。
8. 青龙峡山峰平缓低矮，漫山皆是枣树、栗子树等野生植物，谷底遍是奇形怪状的灵石。
9. 这种贬低自己的比喻，或许能博得同情，却无法给人好感。
10. 贫困治理必须从实际出发，科学研判制约减贫和发展的瓶颈因素，找准释放减贫动力的突破口，因时因势因地制宜，不断调整创新减贫的策略方略和政策工具，提高贫困治理效能。

参考译文与简析

1. Millions of urban residents who have been entitled to free medical care will have to pay part of their medical expenses.（原文是主述结构，应转译为主谓结构，即 residents 作主语，will have to pay 作谓语。）
2. Wang Lie, a generous and learned man, enjoyed a better reputation than Guan Ning and Bing Yuan.（原句中显然不是动词作谓语，属于主述结构，应转译为英语的主谓结构，把最后一部分作为谓语，"器度宽宏，学业精深"译为同位语。）
3. In Hangzhou and other 12 comprehensive pilot zones of cross-border e-commerce, a regulatory system with six subsystems and two platforms as the core has been set up, their successful practices in 12 aspects having been promoted throughout the country.（原文是主述结构，译文中将"杭州等13个跨境电子商务综合试验区"

作地点状语，英语句子转译为主谓结构，使用被动语态。）

4. The Yunmeng Mountain Park, a renowned national forest park in Beijing, has wonderful natural scenery made up of rocky mountains, spectacular waterfalls and lush trees, flowers and grass.（该句小分句较多，每一部分都属于主述结构，经过分析后，主结构为"云蒙山……自然风景十分优美"，其他部分变成从属结构。）

5. China will prosper only when the world prospers, and vice versa.（两部分都是主述结构，转译为英语主谓结构，且第二个分句简化处理。）

6. Information application in rural and remote areas is improved.（原文是主述结构，转译为主谓结构，使用被动语态。）

7. On the banks of the Wuxi section of the Grand Canal, which is narrow and deep, stand rows of traditional houses with grey-tiled roofs and white walls.（原文两部分均为主述结构，将后半部分作主结构，译成主谓结构，"又窄又深"变成定语。）

8. The Qinglong Canyon has a relatively smooth slope covered with wild plants such as date trees and chestnut trees. At the bottom of the canyon is a fascinating landscape made up of rocks.（原文每一部分均为主述结构，拆译为两句话，均为主谓结构。）

9. Through this self-depreciating comparison, he might win sympathy but no favour at all.（原文是伪主谓结构，即主述结构，转译为 he 作主语的主谓结构。）

10. To achieve success in reducing poverty, a country must follow a path in line with its national conditions, identify and remove obstacles to poverty alleviation and development, find driving forces for this cause, and constantly adjust and reform its strategies and policies as circumstances and local conditions change.（原文的"贫困治理"是目的，不是主语，所以英译文要找到真正的主语，即 a country，后面是并列的谓语动词。）

第四章　中文无主句的翻译

前面两章已经提到，中文还有一种句子没有主语，往往以动词开头，这种句子叫作无主句。这种无主句与祈使句不同，一般用来陈述事实，有的使用客观、科学、公正的语气，有的表达一种微妙的情感，有的则是约定俗称的谚语。但由于英文的句式结构一般都是主谓结构，因此，无主句翻译成英文时需要变为主谓结构，一种是英文的主动语态，另一种则是英文的被动语态。至于选择哪种语态的主谓结构，要根据无主句的语气决定。

一、译成英文主动语态的主谓结构，添加主语

首先，中文的政府文件中经常使用无主句，很多时候是一连串的动词短语，但没有说出动作的发出者。这些无主句翻译成英语时最好添加主语 we，有时使用 China。请看下面的例子。

◇ 例 1

要加快完善社会主义市场经济体制，坚决破除各方面体制机制弊端，激发全社会创新创业活力。

We should improve the system of socialist market economy, break down institutional obstacles in all areas, and stimulate the vitality of the whole society in innovation and entrepreneurship.

◇ 例 2

支持港澳防控疫情、发展经济、改善民生，更好融入国家发展大局，保持香港、澳门长期繁荣稳定。

We will help Hong Kong and Macao respond to Covid-19, develop their economies, and improve the well-being of their people, seeing that these two regions better integrate themselves into the country's overall development, and maintain their long-term prosperity and stability.

◇ 例3

要充分发挥中央和地方两个积极性，尊重人民群众首创精神，防止政策执行"一刀切"、层层加码，持续为基层减负。

We will keep the local and central governments fully motivated and respect the pioneering spirit of the people. *We* will avoid a one-size-fits-all approach, avoid making local governments take excessive steps in policy implementation, and continue easing the burdens on those working on the ground.

以上三个例子的原文均为无主句，翻译成英文时均添加主语we。例3根据原文的意群拆成了两句话，第二句依然使用we作主语，和前文保持连贯。

◇ 例4

将扶贫开发与水土保持、环境保护、生态建设相结合，通过生态扶贫、农村人居环境整治、生态脆弱地区易地扶贫搬迁等措施，贫困地区生态保护水平明显改善，守护了绿水青山、换来了金山银山。

China has integrated development-driven poverty alleviation with soil and water conservation and eco-environmental conservation. By developing the eco-economy, improving the rural living environment, and relocating the impoverished from inhospitable areas to places with better economic prospects, *the country* has seen remarkable improvements in the environment of poverty-stricken areas. Lucid waters and lush mountains have become their invaluable assets.

例4原文比较长，根据意群拆分成了三句话，第一句主语使用China，第二句使用了China的上义词country作主语，这样避免了重复，同时又很好地保持了英文的连贯。最后一部分单独译成一句话，一方面表示强调，另一方面可以保证前一句不会太长。

其次，中文谚语往往不必指明动作的发出者，其暗含的主语泛指"人们"。这类句子翻译时可根据情况添加泛指主语 one 或 we，或者译成英文的 there be 结构。有些也可以使用 he 加 who 引导的定语从句作主语。请看下面的例子。

◇ 例 5

活到老，学到老。

译文 1：*One* is never too old to learn.

译文 2：*We* are never too old to learn.

◇ 例 6

留得青山在，不怕没柴烧。

译文 1：As long as there are green mountains, *one / we* need not worry about firewood.

译文 2：Where *there is* life, *there is* hope.

◇ 例 7

不入虎穴，焉得虎子。

译文 1：It is impossible to get the tiger cubs if *one* does not enter the tiger's lair.

译文 2：It is impossible to succeed if *one* makes no efforts.

译文 3：*He* who does not enter the tiger's lair will never get the tiger cubs.

当然，无主句的谚语译成英文时也可添加主语 you。

◇ 例 8

种瓜得瓜，种豆得豆。

译文 1：If *you* have sown melons, *you* will harvest melons while if *you* have sown beans, *you* will harvest beans.

译文 2：*One* will harvest what *he / she* has sown. / As *you* sow, so *you* will reap.

从上面的例子可以看出，中文的谚语、俗语等如果是无主句，有多种主语可以使用。

一些旅游材料中也会使用无主句，表示游客都可以看到或欣赏到一些事物。请看下面的例子。

◇ 例 9

在滑雪的过程中，不仅能感受到绿意盎然的南国风情，还能尽情地享受速度带来的乐趣。

While skiing and appreciating the greenness typical of south China, *visitors/ you* can enjoy to their / your hearts' content the thrill of speed.

◇ 例 10

待到春和景明，望小小空竹斗转在天地乾坤之间，听丝竹音韵萦绕在过耳东风之中，此意美哉。

In mild spring, *it* is fun to watch a diabolo spinning and listen to it whistling in the gentle breeze.

◇ 例 11

在工作繁忙之余来到这里，亲近大自然并享受滑雪乐趣，彻底放松身心。

It is a great choice to take time off work and come to nature, having fun in skiing and relaxing the body and mind.

以上三个例子均来自旅游材料，均为无主句，翻译成英文时使用主动语态，有的使用 visitors 或者 you 作主语，有的使用 it 作形式主语，动词不定式作真正的主语。

二、表示"存现"的无主句译成英文主动语态，用存现的人或物作主语

中文有一种特殊句型叫作存现句，即表示事物存在、出现或消失的句子。一

一般说来，中文的存现句中表示存在、出现或消失的人或事物的名词位于动词之后。有时存现句前面还有表示人或事物存在、出现或消失的处所，如"葫芦架下摆着一张小桌"，这种句子可以归为前一章提及的主述句，但有些中文存现句不出现存在、出现或消失的处所，这种存现句往往是无主句。翻译此类无主句时，可以将原文存现的人或物作主语，有时可使用 there be / occur / exist... 句型。

◇ 例 12

有很多人站在雨里等待结果。

译文 1：*Many people were standing* in the rain waiting for the result.

译文 2：*There were many people standing* in the rain waiting for the result.

◇ 例 13

在环境保护方面，还存在不少问题。

译文 1：With regard to environmental protection, *many problems still exist*.

译文 2：With regard to environmental protection, *there still exist many problems*.

◇ 例 14

突然钻出一只狗，追着她咬，几乎把她吓糊涂了。

译文 1：*Suddenly a dog occurred* and chased after her, scaring her almost out of her wits.

译文 2：*There suddenly occurred a dog* which chased after her and scared her almost out of her wits.

以上三个例子中的原文均为表示存现的无主句，其英译文中基本都将原文中存在或出现的人或物译作主语，或使用正常语序，或用 there be / exist / occur... 等倒装句。

三、译成含被动语态的英文主谓结构

首先，中文的一些科技材料或法律条文经常使用无主句，使表达的内容显得更加客观、科学、公正。这种情况下的无主句译为英文的主谓结构时，一般都转化成被动语态，也就是使用原文的宾语作主语，因为被动语态不强调动作的发出者，更能准确地传达出原文客观、科学、公正的语气，从而实现原文的语用效果。

◇ 例 15

在海拔 3000 米的高空采集到了这种空气样本。

This air sample has been collected at the altitude of 3,000 meters.

◇ 例 16

要制造飞机，就要考虑空气阻力问题。

Air resistance has to be taken into consideration in airplane manufacturing.

◇ 例 17

用机械加工的方法，特别是用磨削的方法，可以获得最佳表面光洁度。

Best surface finish is provided by means of machining, especially by means of grinding.

◇ 例 18

为了防范和惩治恐怖活动，加强反恐怖主义工作，维护国家安全、公共安全和人民生命财产安全，根据宪法，制定本法。

For purposes of preventing and punishing terrorist activities, improving counterterrorism work, and safeguarding national security, public security and the security of people's lives and property, this Law is developed in accordance with the Constitution.

◇ 例 19

禁止携带宠物进入剧院。

No pet is permitted into the theatre.

以上例子分别属于科技文体（例 15、例 16 和例 17）和法律文体（例 18 和例19），为了保留原文客观、科学、公正的语用效果，英译文使用了含被动语态的主谓结构。

其次，中文无主句有时用于表达一种微妙的情感，尤其可以使人在不强调施事者是谁的情况下，表达自己的不满、建议、希望等。英文中遇到同样情况时，通常使用被动语态，这样，说话人或者作者就可以避免对自己所说的话承担责任，听话人或读者也不会感到对方在把他的主观意志强加给自己。所以，中文的此类无主句可以译为英文的被动句。请看下面的例子。

◇ 例 20

为什么总把这些麻烦事推给我呢？

Why are these troubles always left to me?

◇ 例 21

建议直接反映到主管部门去。

It is suggested that the matter be reported directly to competent authorities.

◇ 例 22

由于用餐人数较多，餐位有限，建议尽早预订。

It is recommended that reservation be made as early as possible since there are so many customers and limited tables.

以上三个例子分别表示不满和建议，翻译时均使用了含被动语态的主谓结构。另外，如果中文的无主句以"应该""必须""可以""需要"等能愿动词开头，实际上也表达一种感情色彩，因此，翻译时也可译成使用被动语态的主谓结构。

◇ 例 23

更重要的是，应该给国民经济注入新的活力。

More importantly, fresh impetus should be given to the national economy.

◇ 例 24

必须承认，中国还是一个发展中国家。

It must be recognized that China is still a developing country.

◇ 例 25

紧急情况下，需要对病人采取急救措施。

First aid is needed for patients in case of emergency.

◇ 例 26

决不能把个人利益置于国家利益之上。

Personal interest must not be placed over and above national interest.

当然，中文还有些无主句是因为叙述者使用了第一人称，而且前文已经有了主语"我"，所以下文不必说出，这时便可以根据上下文添加主语 I。

◇ 例 27

在济宁，意外地得知李白竟也是在济宁住过了二十余年啊！

In Jining, I was surprised to learn that Li Bai had lived there for over two decades.

◇ 例 28

有时在夕阳明灭、返映着湖水的时候，我却常常一个人跑到湖边僻静处去乘凉。一边散步，一边听着青蛙在草中奏着雨后之歌，看看小鸟啁啾着向柳枝上飞跳，还觉有些兴致。

Sometimes, when the setting sun was reflected in the water, I would find a quiet place by the lake. While strolling there, I would somewhat enjoy listening to the frogs singing in the grass after the rain and watching twittering birds hopping onto the willow branches.

当然，以上仅是总结了中文无主句翻译的一般规律，任何规律都有例外，所以翻译时可能还会遇到一些无主句不属于本章所述的情况。但无论怎样，中文的无主句一定要译成英文的主谓结构，至于主语的选择要根据语气以及上下文决定。请再看一个例子。

◆ 例 29

移动互联时代，只要连接了网络，就一定会留下痕迹，这些痕迹量化得越精准，对广告主而言越有价值，其可以借助这些数据来分析用户、分析市场。

In the era of mobile interconnection, as long as you are connected to the Internet, you will leave traces. The more precisely these traces are quantified, the more valuable they are to advertisers, who can use these data to analyze the customers and the market.

拓展练习

翻译下列句子，请注意使用英文的主谓结构。

1. 在祭扫时，给坟墓铲除杂草，添加新土，供上祭品，举行简单的祭祀仪式，为已逝的亲人、祖先庄重地送上自己的思念与敬意。
2. 通过祭祀祖先可以追根溯源，从而更好地教育后代，也可以团结海内外华人华侨，增强中华民族的凝聚力。
3. 要在全社会营造尊师重教的良好氛围，让教师成为令人羡慕的职业。
4. 处理好政府和市场的关系，使市场在资源配置中起决定性作用，更好发挥政府作用，构建高水平社会主义市场经济体制。
5. 深入推进公平竞争政策实施，加强反垄断和反不正当竞争，维护公平有序的市场环境。
6. 在新的历史时期，要继续发扬尊老爱幼、勤俭节约等中华民族的优良传统。
7. 明知山有虎，偏向虎山行。
8. 读书破万卷，下笔如有神。
9. 站在山顶，极目远眺，天地浑然一体，宛若仙境。
10. 开展专业志愿服务活动，应当执行国家或者行业组织制定的标准和规程。

参考译文与简析

1. While sweeping tombs, *we* pull up weeds, top up the earth and make offerings in a simple sacrificial ceremony to extend our missing of our ancestors and relatives who have passed away.（原文为无主句，需要根据句意添加主语，无法确定主语时可以添加泛指主语 one、you、we、they、people 等。）

2. By making offerings to our ancestors, *we* can trace back our family roots and better educate future generations. *The day* also brings Chinese speakers around the world closer.（整句话是无主句，可以考虑拆句，译成两个英语主谓句，前面一句用 we 作主语，后半部分"也可以团结……的凝聚力"的主语不应该是 we，而是用 the day 作主语。）

3. *We* should build up the social norms of respecting teachers and valuing education to make teaching a job admired by all.（译成用 we 作主语的主谓结构，符合原文的语气。）

4. To develop a high-standard socialist market economy, *we* should deal well with the relationship between the government and the market, seeing that the market plays the decisive role in the allocation of resources and the government better fulfills its role.（原文均为动词短语，翻译前应进行分析，找到主结构，即"处理好政府和市场的关系"，译成 we 作主语的主谓结构，把"构建高水平社会主义市场经济体制"变成目的状语前置，将"使市场在资源配置中起决定性作用，更好发挥政府作用"变成现在分词作状语。）

5. *We* will further the implementation of policies to ensure fair competition and take stronger action against monopolies and unfair competition to ensure a well-ordered and fair market environment.（本句可用 we 作主语，后面"维护公平有序的市场环境"作状语。）

6. In the new era, *we* will carry on traditional Chinese virtues like respecting the old and cherishing the young as well as working hard and being frugal.（这里也用 we 作主语，找到主结构，"尊老爱幼、勤俭节约等"变成举例的成分。）

7. *He* who knows there is a tiger in the mountains still goes there. / When it is tough, do it tough.（这句是谚语，可以用 he 作主语，后面跟定语从句。当然，也可以像第二个译文那样，主结构使用祈使句。）

8. *He* who reads extensively is good at writing. / *You* will be good at writing after reading so much.（该句的第一种翻译方法同第七句，第二种翻译使用了 you 作泛指主语。）

9. Standing on the top of the mountain, *you* can enjoy the panoramic view as if *you* were in a wonderland.（这一句选自旅游文本，根据英语同类文体的特点，使用 you 作主语。）

10. To carry out professional voluntary service activities, the standards and procedures developed by the state and industrial organizations shall be implemented.（这一句原文比较客观、正式，所以转译为主谓结构时使用了被动语态。）

第五章　英文定语从句的翻译

中英文定语的位置不同。中文的定语一般放在被修饰词的前面，而且定语一般不会太长。英文句子中的定语如果是单词，则放在被修饰语的前面，如果是短语或者从句，则放在被修饰语的后面。由于中英文的这一区别，翻译时很多人会把定语从句直接译成中文的定语，有时可以这样翻译，但有时译文中的定语则显得冗长。因此，定语从句的翻译也是翻译学习者应该注意的一个方面。

一、前置翻译

首先，如果英文定语从句比较短，而且被修饰词前后没有其他较强的定语修饰成分，翻译时一般将定语从句放在被修饰词的前面。请看下面的例子。

✧ 例 1

Anyone *who has ever visited Switzerland* will tell you that its public transportation service is one of the finest worldwide.

任何<u>到过瑞士</u>的人都会告诉您，瑞士公共交通服务堪称世界一流。

✧ 例 2

Another area *where women of Cyprus have been very active* for the past 29 years, but more so in recent years, is the area of peace.

过去 29 年，<u>塞浦路斯妇女活跃于和平领域</u>，近年来更为活跃。

✧ 例 3

Small businesses *that are considering purchasing or selling online* will find this a useful resource to help them identify and select appropriate e-commerce options.

正在考虑在线购买或销售的小型企业将会发现这是一个有用的资源，可以帮助他们识别并选择合适的电子商务选项。

◆ 例 4

In some countries *where primary education is not yet universal*, however, such as Bangladesh and Nepal, the share of primary education has nevertheless fallen since 1999.

但是，在初等教育还不普及的一些国家（如孟加拉国和尼泊尔），1999 年以来初等教育的份额已经下降。

以上例子中原文斜体部分都是限定性定语从句，其所修饰的词前后都没有其他修饰成分，而且定语从句都很短，翻译时直接译为中文的定语。

其次，英文中有些非限定性定语从句很短，而且非限定性定语从句中动词表示的动作发生在主句动词动作之前或者同时发生，这样的非限定性定语从句可以翻译成前置的定语。

◆ 例 5

A visit to Aarau Castle, *which houses the city museum*, is practically essential before leaving town.

离开小镇之前，一定不要错过参观城市博物馆所在地阿劳城堡。

◆ 例 6

The Mexican revolution, *which had first broken out in 1910*, was just over, and there was a will to rebuild the country.

爆发于 1910 年的墨西哥革命当时已经结束，人们渴望重建家园。

◆ 例 7

Perhaps this is the "death ray", *which we often read about in science fiction.*

也许这就是我们常在科幻小说中读到的"死光"。

这三个例子中的非限定性定语从句很短，其中例 5 和例 6 的定语从句中动词表示的动作发生在主句动词动作之前，例 7 的定语从句的动作和主结构中动词的动作基本同步。三个例子的定语从句均译为前置定语。当然，这几个非限定性定语从句也可以放在原文所在的位置，即后置翻译。

二、融合翻译

如果英文句子的主句是 There be... 结构或 This is... 结构，后面的名词跟一个限定性定语从句，翻译时可以将主句和从句进行融合翻译。请看下面的例子。

✧ 例 8

There are many people *who want to see the film*.
许多人想看这部电影。

✧ 例 9

In the natural surroundings of Graubünden, there are also many instances *where relaxed moments prevail over the hustle and bustle, allowing you to appreciate the simple things in life*.
在格劳宾登州的自然环境中，很多情况下恬静胜过了喧嚣，使人们得以欣赏生活中的简单事物。

✧ 例 10

This is the very laser scalpel *which he used to operate on a patient suffering from malignant tumor*.
他就是用这把激光刀给一位恶性肿瘤患者动手术的。

以上三个例子的定语从句翻译时均与主句融合，中文显得很通顺。

三、后置翻译

所谓后置翻译，就是指翻译时将定语从句放置在被修饰语的后面，与前面的分句构成并列关系，一般需要在后一分句（即定语从句的中译文）开头重复一下先行词，也可使用人称代词和指示代词（"这""那""这里""那里"等）引出该分句，当然个别情况下，如果前后比较紧凑，则无须重复名词或使用代词。

首先，一些限定性定语从句本身虽然较短，但是先行词前后往往还有其他较强的修饰成分，譬如先行词前面有形容词修饰，后面有介词短语或分词短语修饰，这样的限定性定语从句需要后置翻译。

◇ 例 11

The valley was a great lake, reaching to the big trees in the fields *which had not yet lost the fire in their branches.*

河谷俨然一片浩瀚的湖泽，一直漫延到田野中的大树，大树的枝丫间还留有天火的余烬。

◇ 例 12

Most ranches are located in flat open country *where there is plenty of grass for the cattle to feed on.*

大多数牧场位于平坦开阔的地区，那里有充足的青草可供放牧。

以上两个例子中原文斜体部分是限定性定语从句，其所修饰的词均有其他修饰成分修饰，如例 11 原文中的 trees 前面是 big，后面是 in the fields，例 12 原文中的 country 前面是 flat 和 open 两个形容词。这两个定语从句如果再译到被修饰词前面的话，就会显得冗长，因此，需要后置翻译。

其次，限定性定语从句本身结构比较复杂冗长，如果译成中文的前置定语会显得很长，超出了中文定语的"度"，不符合中文的表达习惯。这类定语从句也需要译成后置结构。

◇ 例13

Lotteries are games of chance *in which individuals are sold tickets, giving them the opportunity to win a drawing of cash or some other prize.*

彩票是机会游戏,<u>个人购买彩票,有机会赢得一笔现金或其他奖品</u>。

◇ 例14

China has developed up to 53 "high-tech industry development zones" *which have contributed to the rapid growth of China's high-tech activities.*

中国已建起53个"高科技工业开发区",<u>为中国高科技产业的快速发展作出了贡献</u>。(或:中国已建起53个"高科技工业开发区",<u>有力地推动了中国高科技产业的快速发展</u>。)

◇ 例15

It is easiest to see this in the craftsman *who lovingly shapes some cheap material into an object that may be either useful or beautiful or both.*

这一点最容易在工匠身上看出来,<u>他总是深情地将某种廉价材料做成一件或有用或美观或两者兼备的东西</u>。

以上三个例子中,原文的定语从句虽然是限定性定语从句,但是这些定语从句本身比较长,如果译到被修饰词的前面,会显得定语过于冗长,因此采取后置翻译,将定语从句译成小分句放在主句后面,显得非常通顺。

第三,有些限定性定语从句中的动作发生在主句中的动作之后,这样的定语从句最好也采取后置翻译法。请看下面的例子。

◇ 例16

In a few minutes the streams were caught up, rejoicing, in the embrace of the deep river *which would carry them with it to the sea.*

再过几分钟,这些小溪就会欢快地投入大河的怀抱,<u>一起奔向大海</u>。

◇ 例 17

Enjoying a prime location, the hotel can also promise you a soft, comfortable bed *in which to rest your weary bones.*

酒店地理位置优越，床铺柔软舒适，<u>供您放松疲惫的身体</u>。

◇ 例 18

Governments and NGOs in countries with high rates of HIV-prevalence have introduced measures *that support the educational needs of orphans.*

艾滋病毒感染率高的国家中，政府和非政府组织已经采取措施，<u>满足孤儿的教育需求</u>。

仔细阅读以上三个例子的原文不难看出，定语从句中的动词表示的动作发生在主句动词表示的动作之后，因此，不宜将这样的限定性定语从句翻译成中文的定语，而是后置，使其成为与主句并列的结构，体现先后顺序。

第四，大多数非限定性定语从句一般都可以采用"后置法"进行翻译，因为非限定性定语从句一般表示对被修饰词的补充说明，没有很强的修饰作用，翻译时将其后置比较符合中文的表达习惯。当然，和限定性定语从句一样，有时要重复一下英文句子中的先行词，有时要使用人称代词或指示代词，有时则可省略，视具体情况而定。

◇ 例 19

The U.S. Constitution, which was drafted in 1787 and adopted in 1788, is the oldest written constitution still in effect.

《美国宪法》<u>起草于 1787 年，于 1788 年生效</u>，是仍在生效的最古老宪法。

◇ 例 20

The story goes that his godfather, *who used to run the hotel,* would go for walks with the little animals in the morning hours.

据说他的教父<u>曾经营过一家酒店</u>，早上会和小动物们一起散步。

◇ 例 21

The tints in the sky were wonderful, every conceivable shade of blue-grey, *which contrived to modulate into the golden brilliance in which the sun was veiled.*

空中的色彩美妙绝伦，呈各种深浅不一的蓝灰色，这些蓝灰色竭力幻化成一片金色光辉，给太阳蒙上了面纱。

◇ 例 22

The absolute high spot is the grand firework display to music, *which lights up the Davos sky after darkness has fallen.*

真正的高潮是盛大的音乐焰火表演，夜幕降临后，五彩缤纷的焰火将照亮达沃斯的夜空。

◇ 例 23

Our hero is Yossarian, a bombardier with the 256th Squadron, *which is engaged in bombing southern France and Italy.*

主人公尤索林是第 256 中队的投弹手，该中队主要负责轰炸法国南部和意大利。

◇ 例 24

Macroeconomics is the study of the national economy as a whole, *which considers the operation condition, the future trend and the interrelationship of the internal components in a broad sense.*

宏观经济学以整个国民经济作为研究对象，考察总体经济的运行状况、发展趋势和内部各个组成部分之间的相互关系。

以上例子中，定语从句均为非限定性定语从句，翻译时均放在了原文定语从句的位置，相对于被修饰的词来说，这些定语从句的译文均属于后置，即定语从句的译文均放在了被修饰词的后面。

当然，英文中不少定语从句，包括限定性和非限定性定语从句（特别是非限定性定语从句），在形式上虽然用作定语，但在意义上与主句存在一定的逻辑关系，说明时间、原因、让步、条件或目的等，这要求译者善于从原文的字里行间读出其中的逻辑关系，然后翻译成中文相应的偏正复句，即因果、假设、转折等复句。请看下面的例子。

◇ 例25

The development of China's high-tech parks from 1988 to 1997 was mainly planned by top governmental officials *who were clearly influenced by existing models such as Silicon Valley in the US, Tsukuba in Japan, or Hsinchu Science Park in Taiwan.*

1988年到1997年间中国高科技园的开发主要由政府高层官员规划，<u>而这些人明显受到美国硅谷、日本筑波、台湾省新竹工业园等已有模式的影响</u>。

◇ 例26

In some of them (Ethiopia, India and Uganda are examples), *where there is experience of sectorwide programmes going back as far as ten years*, evidence of many of the principles in the Paris indicators already exists.

其中有些国家（譬如埃塞俄比亚、印度和乌干达），<u>由于各部门的计划已经有长达十年的经验</u>，所以已经存在可以证明巴黎宣言指标中诸多原则的证据。

◇ 例27

This applies particularly to the Asian least developed countries (LDCs) that border China and *that hope to emulate its success and exploit the opportunities presented by this growing demand for foreign goods.*

这尤其适用于与中国接壤的亚洲最不发达国家（LDCs），<u>因为这些国家希望效仿中国的成功，并能利用中国日益增长的对外商品需求所带来的机遇</u>。

◇ 例28

Nevertheless, its key targets were the developed markets of Japan, the US, and the European Union, *where it was necessary to get around the difficulty of current or the potential protective barriers.*

但是，其主要目标瞄准了日本、美国和欧盟的成熟市场，<u>不过，在这些国家，需要克服现有或潜在的保护壁垒</u>。

以上几个例子中的定语从句有限定性的，但大部分是非限定性的，翻译成后置成分时根据句子意思，中文加上了一些表示前后逻辑关系的词。

以上是英文定语从句的译法，不难看出，大多数情况下，译者要考虑到中英文定语位置的差异，将定语从句进行调整，或后置，或融合，或根据前后逻辑关系转译为表示因果、转折、条件或目的的偏正复句。希望本章总结出的一些规律可以给读者一些启示，这样在翻译中可以避免一部分拗口的欧化句式。

拓展练习

翻译下列句子，请注意英语定语从句的翻译。

1. Tourism is a particularly globalized industry, *where making a strong commitment to sustainability is becoming increasingly important.*
2. In 2015, Zurich Tourism reinvigorated this commitment with the development of the comprehensive Sustainability Concept 2015+, *which set credible and ambitious goals for the coming years.*
3. Most of the countries *for which data are available* allocated less than 50% of their total education expenditure to primary education in 2004.
4. This fund finances local projects *that reduce CO_2 emissions* while at the same time strengthening local suppliers and businesses, conserving local resources and offering guests and customers high-quality products and experiences.
5. We offset any remaining emissions in projects *that actively and measurably remove CO_2 from the atmosphere.*
6. On the initiative of the destination organization, tourism businesses, event organizers and trade are participating in an initiative *that reduces and offsets the*

climate effects of their activities.

7. There were men in that crowd *who had stood there every day for a month.*

8. The whole country is classified into Provinces, Autonomous Regions, Municipalities, and Special Administrative Regions, all *of which are province level divisions, which are also the highest-level divisions under the direct management of Central People's Government.*

9. Victorinox produces and sells unique, high quality products worldwide *which are of practical use in differing areas of life.*

10. Besides the "traditional" women's organizations and trade unions, most *of which are affiliated to political parties and have a very general mandate*, there are many other specialized organizations, non-political, focused on a specific target/goal.

参考译文与简析

1. 旅游业属于特别全球化的行业，<u>因此对可持续发展做出坚定承诺变得日益重要</u>。（原句中 where 引导的非限定性定语从句在译文中后置，根据前后的逻辑关系，译文中添加"因此"二字。）

2. 2015 年，苏黎世旅游局通过制定全面的 2015+ 可持续发展理念来重申这一承诺，<u>为未来几年树立了切实而宏大的目标</u>。（原文中 which 引导的非限定性定语从句在译文中后置，与前面主句并列。）

3. <u>能获得数据的</u>大多数国家 2004 年分配到初等教育的支出不超过教育总支出的 50%。（原文中 which 引导的限定性定语从句比较短，翻译时放在定语的位置即可。）

4. 该基金为<u>减少二氧化碳排放的</u>当地项目提供资金，促进当地供应商和企业发展，保护当地资源，并为客户提供高质量的产品和体验。（该句中 that 引导的限定性定语从句很短，翻译时译成中文的定语即可，while 后面的状语部分依次译成中文的并列结构。）

5. 我们抵消了<u>那些积极从大气中清除大量二氧化碳的项目中</u>剩余的排放量。（本句中 that 引导的限定性定语从句译成中文的定语即可。）

6. 在该目的地组织的倡议下，旅游企业、活动组织者和行业参与了一个项目，<u>旨在减少和抵消其活动对气候的影响</u>。（原文中的限定性定语从句较长，而且意思上与主句之间形成了目的关系，所以翻译时后置，并添加"旨在"二字表示目的。)

7. 人群中有些人每天站在那里，站了一个月。(该句原文使用了 there be 结构，翻译时将定语从句和主句融合处理，显得更通顺。)

8. 全国分为省、自治区、直辖市和特别行政区，四者皆属省级行政区域，也是中央人民政府直接管辖下的最高行政单位。(原文中的两个定语从句均是非限定性的，翻译时均后置即可。)

9. 维氏在全球范围内生产、销售独具特色的高品质产品，适用于生活的方方面面。(原文中限定性定语从句所修饰的名词 products 前面还有很强的修饰成分，即 "unique, high quality products" 这一部分，因此翻译时定语从句需后置。)

10. 大多数"传统"的妇女组织和工会隶属于某些政党，完成非常宽泛的任务。除此之外，还有不少专门组织，不属于任何政党，专注于实现某一特定目的或目标。(此处为非限定性定语从句，但根据句子含义，翻译时需与前面部分进行融合处理。)

第六章　英文同位语的翻译

中英文背后的思维不同，因此，中英文在语言方面有很多不同，其中一个不同就在于语序不同，而语序的不同之一表现在同位语的不同。英文的同位语有几种形式，本章将分类详细讲解英文同位语的翻译。

一、"名词 + 名词（短语）"同位语

"名词 + 名词（短语）"是英语中最常见的同位语形式，后面的名词前后用逗号或者破折号分开。这类同位语一般有以下几种译法。

（一）译成中文"职务/功能或地位 + 人名/地名"的形式

英语中有些同位语前面的名词一般是人名或地名，后面是人的职务或地方的功能。这类同位语翻译成中文时一般将职务放在前面，人名或地名放在后面，以符合中文的习惯。请看下面的例子。

◇ 例 1

Naomi Varnis, an African Studies student at Brown, doesn't believe the novel is a groundbreaking commentary on race.

布朗大学非洲研究专业的学生内奥米·瓦尼斯并不认为该小说在探讨种族问题方面具有开创性。

◇ 例 2

Davos—the highest-altitude town in Europe—offers all the amenities of a small town, yet at the same time it is surrounded by an intact natural landscape and a marvellous mountain world.

欧洲海拔最高的小镇达沃斯四周是纯净的自然美景和壮观的高山世界，小镇设施一应俱全。

以上两个例子中，例1的同位语就是人名后面跟身份，例2的同位语是地名后面跟地方的功能/地位，翻译时根据中文的习惯将职务或功能/地位提前，后面再加人名或地名，去掉同位语的逗号或破折号。这样的译文显得通顺且地道。

当然，英文有些句子中也会把职位放在人名的前面，这种情况直接按照原文顺序翻译即可。

◇ 例3

Volkswagen(VW) AG Chairman Ferdinand Piech poured cold water on the current craze for mergers and acquisitions in the auto sector—a trend the German car maker itself encouraged with no fewer than three acquisitions in the past year alone.

大众汽车集团董事长费尔南多·皮耶希给汽车行业的并购热泼了冷水。大众汽车本身去年一年就进行了三次并购，助长了并购行为。

（二）译成中文的判断句

有些名词同位语如果比较长，可以译为中文的判断句。请看下面的例子。

◇ 例4

Almost all of the 50 affluent parents in and around New York City that I interviewed expressed fears that children would be "*entitled*" —*a dirty word that meant, variously, lazy, materialistic, greedy, rude, selfish and self-satisfied.*

我采访了纽约内外50位富裕的家长，他们几乎都表示害怕孩子会觉得自己"享有特权"（entitled）。"享有特权"这个词不是一个好词，有很多意思，包括"懒惰""贪图享乐""贪婪""粗鲁""自私"和"自满"。

◇ 例5

Few Web sites generated as much media buzz in 2005 as *Wikipedia, the collectively authored online encyclopedia.*

<u>维基百科是集体编纂的在线百科</u>。2005 年，几乎没有网站能像维基百科那样引发媒体如此关注。

◇ 例 6

Otto Wagner (1841—1918), the most successful architect in turn-of-the-century Vienna, gained lasting importance as an organizer of large-scale projects.

<u>奥托·瓦格纳（1841—1918）是世纪之交维也纳最成功的建筑师</u>，作为一些大规模项目的组织者，瓦格纳的重要地位名垂青史。

以上三个例子的原文中，例 4 中的 a dirty word that meant, variously, lazy, materialistic, greedy, rude, selfish and self-satisfied 是 entitled 的同位语，例 5 中 the collectively authored online encyclopedia 是 Wikipedia 的同位语，例 6 中 the most successful architect in turn-of-the-century Vienna 是 Otto Wagner (1841—1918) 的同位语。这些同位语均较长，如果直接译成前面所讲的中文同位语形式，会显得冗长，因此要考虑译成判断句。

（三）融合法

有些"名词 + 名词（短语）"结构的同位语，考虑到中译文的通顺，也可以将两者融合翻译，特别是前后名词之间是包含与被包含的关系时。请看下面的例子。

◇ 例 7

People who lack genuine core values rely on *external factors—their looks or status*—in order to feel good about themselves.

缺乏真正核心价值观的人依赖<u>长相或地位等外部因素</u>，从而让自己感觉良好。

◇ 例 8

In *Graubünden, a region* of harsh mountain ranges, idyllic alps and crystal-clear lakes, patgific is a way of life for the easy-going locals.

格劳宾登地区拥有连绵起伏的山脉、如诗如画的阿尔卑斯山和水晶般清澈的湖泊，当地人平易近人，恬淡安逸是他们的一种生活方式。

◇ 例 9

*These countries—Afghanistan, Bhutan, Lao People's Democratic Republic, Myanmar and Nepal—*have high-quality produce and unique goods for which viable market niches could be developed in China, accessible through e-commerce market places.

这些国家包括阿富汗、不丹、老挝人民民主共和国、缅甸和尼泊尔。他们拥有高质量的产品和独特的商品，并且这些产品和商品容易通过电子商务市场进入中国市场，在中国发展切实可行的市场利基。

以上三个例子原文的斜体部分均为同位语，而且每一组同位语均为包含和被包含的关系，翻译时两者应进行融合。

（四）顺序不变

有些名词短语作同位语，用来解释说明某一情况，翻译时不必调整顺序，直接放在所在的位置即可。请看下面的例子。

◇ 例 10

Industries ranging from automobiles to energy to housing are grappling with a common environmental *theme: going green.*

从汽车、能源到住房等行业都在努力推动一个共同的环境主题：绿色环保。

◇ 例 11

The first pieces of economic data to be published in January—*the purchasing managers' indices (PMI) for the manufacturing sector*—were pretty upbeat.

1 月份发布的首批经济数据——制造业采购经理人指数（PMI）相当乐观。

以上两个例子中，例 10 中的 going green 是同位语，是对前面名词 theme 的补充；例 11 中的 the purchasing managers' indices (PMI) for the manufacturing sector 是同位语，也是对前面 the first pieces of economic data 的补充说明，翻译时直接放在所在位置即可。

二、"名词 +of+ 名词（短语）"同位语

英文中的介词 of 大多数情况下表示所属关系，但有些情况下表示同位关系，即 of 后面的部分是对前面名词的补充或解释，而前面的词一般是 idea、concept 等。这种同位语的翻译比较简单，可以译为"……这一想法 / 观点 / 概念"等。请看下面的例子。

◇ 例 12

This concept of Shared Prosperity is aligned to Malaysia's global and domestic aspirations.

"共同繁荣"这一理念与马来西亚国际和国内目标一致。

◇ 例 13

His current status is enhanced by the use of *his concept of structure of feeling* to study various phenomena from literary texts to urban ways of life.

他使用"感觉结构"这一概念去研究从文学文本到城市生活方式等各种现象，从而巩固了他的当代地位。

◇ 例 14

But *the goal of an insect-free world* continued to recede.

但无害虫的世界这一目标继续渐行渐远。

三、同位语从句

英文还有一种同位语，即同位语从句，一般加在 idea、concept、fact、assumption 等单词的后面，说明这些单词所包含的内容，与这些名词一起构成主

语、宾语、表语等。这种同位语从句一般可以有两种译法：如果同位语和前面的名词一起构成主语，一般先翻译同位语从句的内容，然后再说"这一想法/概念/理念/设想……"；如果同位语和前面的名词一起作宾语，可以先翻译名词，然后再引出同位语从句的内容，有时可能还需要变通一下词性或者做一定的融合处理。请看下面的例子。

◇ 例 15

While there have been substantive critiques of Wikipedia's accuracy and comprehensiveness, *the idea that a free encyclopedia written entirely by volunteers could give the venerable Britannica a run for its money* would have sounded preposterous even 10 years ago.

尽管对维基百科准确性和综合性的批评委实不少，但<u>一部完全由志愿者编写的自由百科全书能够与历史悠久的大英百科全书展开竞争</u>，<u>这种想法甚至十年前听上去还是荒谬的</u>。

◇ 例 16

We have been checking interesting acquisition targets over the past few years and have come to *the conclusion that there wasn't anything worthwhile.*

过去几年，我们一直在审查让人感兴趣的收购目标，得出的<u>结论却是，没有公司值得收购</u>。

◇ 例 17

For the three decades prior to 2008, some countries, including the U.S. and the UK, chose a path that led to greater inequality, often on *the assumption that there was no viable alternative.*

2008 年之前的 30 年间，包括美国和英国在内的部分国家选择了一条通往更不平等的道路，这些国家<u>常常认为没有其他可行的选择</u>。

◇ 例 18

Last is the more general observation *that technological developments are likely to be even more dramatic in the future than they have been in the recent past.*

最后是一种更普遍的看法，即未来的技术可能会比迄今为止的发展更为迅猛。

以上四个例子中，例 15 中 idea 在句子中作主语，翻译时先翻译后面同位语从句的内容，然后再说"这一想法 / 这种想法"。例 16 和例 17 中原文 conclusion 和 assumption 分别作动词短语 come to 和介词 on 的宾语，所以先翻译名词，然后再翻译同位语从句，而且两个例子的译文都做了一定的处理，例 16 加了"却是"，例 17 则将 assumption 转译成了动词，与后面的从句融合。例 18 将同位语从句的翻译放在了最后，用"即"引出。

综上所述，英文同位语的翻译并非仅有一种规则，因为英文的同位语不是一种形式，而是多种形式，特别是前文所讲的第一种形式又有多种不同的翻译方法，因此需要翻译学习者好好把握其中的规律，掌握翻译的原则。当然，掌握了英文同位语的翻译之后，对中译英也会有一定的启发。比如有些中文句子中，一些判断句仅是一个小分句，这时不妨使用同位语。请看两个例子。

◇ **例 19**

中国是发展中国家，在运用现代知识和科学技术等方面已经取得了很大进步，但同发达国家相比，还有很多的差距。

China, a developing country, has made great progress in applying modern knowledge and science and technology, but it has a long way to go in comparison with developed countries.

◇ **例 20**

司马迁是西汉时期的史学家，用十四年的时间完成了中国第一部纪传体通史《史记》，被公认为是中国史书的典范。

Sima Qian, a historian of the Western Han Dynasty, spent fourteen years writing Historical Records, China's first history book in a biographical and thematic style, which is known as a model of Chinese historical books.

拓展练习

翻译下列句子,请注意英文同位语的翻译。

1. The houses built by *the brothers, Charles Sumner Greene (1868—1957) and Henry Mather Greene (1870—1954)*, and the buildings of Bernard Maybeck (1862—1955), tend to strike present-day beholders as willfully idiosyncratic.

2. Women's penetration in the field of the mass media—*a vital field for the promotion of gender issues*—is undisputable.

3. Gothic reflects dark times, too, and offers escapism from austerity or insecurity—*a safe, containable way to be scared*.

4. A life of principle, of not succumbing to *the seductive sirens* of an easy morality, will always win the day.

5. Yet these parents have a problem: *how to give their kids these advantages while also setting limits*.

6. Years later, in 1887, Captain Arthur H. Keller, *a former Confederate officer* who had become a newspaper editor in Tuscumbia, Alabama, brought his six-year-old deaf-blind daughter Helen to Bell in Washington.

7. Otto Wagner, *the leading architect of the Viennese school, and a chief figure in the Vienna Secession*, built the Post Office Savings Bank in Vienna in 1904.

8. Cubism, *the next development in avant-garde art*, in some respects seemed to continue the dialogue began by the Fauves and in some respects seemed to contradict it.

9. The project was predicated on the assumption *that the economy was expanding*.

10. The question *whether we need more time to do the work* has not been decided.

参考译文与简析

1. 查尔斯·萨姆纳·格林(1868 — 1957)和亨利·马瑟·格林(1870 — 1954)兄弟二人建造的房屋和伯纳德·梅贝克(Bernard Maybeck)(1862 — 1955)建造的大楼追求标新立异,给今天的人们留下了深刻的印象。(翻译时对同位语的语序做了调整。)

2. 毫无疑问，大众媒体中的女性从业人数日益增多，而<u>大众媒体正是宣传性别问题的重要领域</u>。（原文中同位语 a vital field for the promotion of gender issues 较长，要考虑译成中文的判断句。）

3. 哥特式小说也是黑暗时期的写照，使人们逃离严苛或不安全的状态，<u>以一种安全可控的方式去感受恐惧</u>。（分析同上。）

4. 有原则地去生活，不受享乐道德观<u>这一女妖</u>的诱惑，就会成功。（the seductive sirens 作 an easy morality 的同位语，译为"享乐道德观这一女妖"。当然，由于"女妖"一词对中国读者来说可能有点陌生，也可以直接译成"享乐人生观"。）

5. 然后，这些家长有一个顾虑：<u>在设定限制的同时，如何让孩子享受这些优越性</u>。（翻译时，原文冒号之后的同位语直接放在译文后面即可。）

6. 几年后，即 1887 年，亚瑟·H·凯勒上尉将自己六岁的聋盲女儿海伦带到华盛顿，见到了贝尔。亚瑟·H·凯勒曾是南部邦联的<u>一名军官</u>，后来在阿拉巴马州的塔斯坎比亚担任报纸编辑。（同位语 a former Confederate officer 后面还跟了定语从句，这部分较长，翻译时可放在后面单独成句，起补充说明作用。）

7. 奥托·瓦格纳是<u>维也纳学派的杰出建筑师，也是维也纳分离派的主要人物</u>，于 1904 年在维也纳建造了邮政储蓄银行。（原文 Otto Wagner 后面的同位语较长，因此译为中文的判断句。）

8. 立体画派是<u>继先锋派之后的又一艺术流派，在某些方面似乎延续了野兽派开创的艺术，但在另一些方面又似乎与之相矛盾</u>。（分析同上。）

9. 这一计划基于<u>经济正在发展</u>这一设想之上。（先翻译 that 引导的同位语从句，再加上"这一设想"。）

10. <u>我们是否需要更多时间来做这项工作</u>，这一问题还没有决定。（同位语 whether we need more time to do the work 在译文中提前，然后将主句译文放在后面。）

第七章　英文形容词变通翻译的几种情况

英文形容词一般放在名词前面作定语，大多数情况下直译即可。但有时候，一个名词前面有多个形容词，如果按照原文的顺序翻译，定语可能会显得冗长。有时候，英文还会用一个由形容词变来的副词修饰一个形容词，共同作定语，如果直接把副词译成副词，形容词译成形容词，译文也会显得比较拗口。这两种情况下，翻译时需要进行一定的变通。下面分别举例说明。

一、英文多个并列形容词的翻译

一般翻译学习者看到英文的形容词就会将之译为"……的"，看到并列的形容词就会按照原文的顺序进行翻译，以至于出现多个"……的"结构，而且会将并列形容词之间的逗号直接译为中文的逗号，这样的翻译实际上并不符合中文的表达习惯。如 longest secured glacier descent 这一短语中有两个形容词，一个是 longest，一个是 secured，如果直接译为"最长的安全的冰川速降滑道"则会显得比较拗口，这时仅需要对其进行简单的调整，译成"带保护设施的最长冰川速降滑道"，则更地道。因此，英文中多个并列形容词的翻译需要根据情况进行变通，或者至少将逗号改为顿号，将部分"的"省略。请看下面的例子。

◇ 例 1

Even *small and remote* locations can be reached by public transport.
即使是<u>偏远的小地方</u>也可以搭乘公共交通工具到达。

◇ 例 2

Where *appropriate and commercially viable*, Interlaken Tourism gives priority to environmentally-friendly transport options, activities and events.

在商业可行的适当情况下，因特拉肯旅游局优先考虑环保的交通选择、活动和赛事。

以上两个例子的原文均使用了两个并列形容词，例1的形容词和后面的名词直接按原文翻译就是"小的和偏远的地方"，例2的形容词直接按原文翻译则是"合适的和商业可行的"，这两个译文显然不通顺，因此需要调整顺序，省略其中一个形容词的"的"字，译文就通顺得多。

◇ 例 3

That is a truly radical break from the *traditional closed-door, credentialed* method of producing Encyclopædia Britannica and its ilk.

这彻底打破了大英百科等百科全书封闭式、经授权的传统编纂方法。

◇ 例 4

Materials have been prepared for tourists in image, word and sound, all of which means the ideas box for *sustainable, concrete and bookable* travel experiences is growing as quickly as the demand.

已经为游客准备了图像、文字和声音等资料，所有这些都意味着可持续、可预订的具体旅行体验创意正在与需求同步快速增长。

例3和例4原文中斜体部分是三个形容词并列，均不能按照原文顺序翻译，而且不能三个形容词都加"的"，需要适当调整，适当省略"的"字，译文会变得更加通顺。

另外，英文中多个形容词并列作定语时，国家名或地域名紧靠所修饰的词，其他词放在外围。但中文往往相反，翻译时需要进行一定的调整。请看下面的例子。

◇ 例 5

These companies benefit from a very favourable environment which includes *strong government* support, a sophisticated network of university-based institutions, and a large pool of well-trained researchers and engineers.

这些公司受益于良好的环境，其中包括政府的大力支持、大学里众多的研究机构以及训练有素的科研人员和工程师。

◇ 例 6

The joint venture provides Huawei with access to the *local Russian* market that it would be extremely difficult for them to penetrate on their own.

该合营公司为华为提供了进入俄罗斯地方市场的机会，如果单靠华为自己，渗透这一市场则非常困难。

例 5 和例 6 中原文 strong government support 和 local Russian market 分别译成了"政府的大力支持"和"俄罗斯地方市场"，显然比按照原文顺序翻译为"大力的政府支持"和"地方俄罗斯市场"要通顺很多，而且逻辑上也比后者清晰。

◇ 例 7

Moreover, developments of technology are likely to force or call for *additional*, *significant*, *and perhaps fundamental* shifts in national attitudes toward both domestic and international affairs.

更有甚者，技术发展可能会迫使或要求各国对国内外事务的态度发生更多重大转变，也许是根本性的转变。

这个例子的原文斜体部分是三个形容词，显然不能按照原文顺序翻译，需要先调整前两个形容词按顺序翻译，但省译"的"字，将后面的 perhaps fundamental 调整到译文的最后，这样处理能使译文更地道。

二、英文"描述性副词 + 形容词"结构的翻译

英文有时会用一个描述性的副词修饰一个形容词，由于这个副词的描述性特别强，如果按照原文的形式进行翻译，译文会显得不通顺。例如将 happily tired 译成"不高兴地疲惫"就会让读者感到很奇怪，不如译作"很疲倦，却又非常高兴"。因此，遇到这种结构，英文的副词也要译成中文的形容词，就是将英文的

副词和后面的形容词均译为中文的形容词。请看下面的例子。

◆ 例 8

Uniquely cool! A car-free vacation paradise.
独一无二，酷爽无比！一个禁止汽车通行的度假天堂。

这个例子中的 uniquely cool 显然不能译成"独特地凉爽/酷爽"，原文的意思是既 unique（独一无二），又 cool（酷爽），译成两个形容词比较通顺。而且根据该句的上下文，可以分别译成四字格，即"独一无二"和"酷爽无比"。

◆ 例 9

He, too, had been reviewing the history of their lives—and had seen her from her childhood to her present age, so sweet, so innocent, so *charmingly simple*, and *artlessly fond* and tender. (*Vanity Fair*)
他（奥斯本）回首往事，看到她从孩童时代变成现在这个青春少女，那么甜美，那么纯真，那么美丽单纯，那么纯朴痴情，那么温良有加。(《名利场》)

◆ 例 10

He was a tall, thin old man with a bald head, which shone *pinkishly dirty*, and a grizzled beard so long he could tuck it in his belt. (*Gone with the Wind*)
这个人瘦高瘦高的，已经上了年纪，留着光头，脏兮兮的，泛着粉色，灰白色的胡子很长，长到可以塞进他的皮带里。(《飘》)

以上两个例子中，斜体部分也是描述性副词加形容词结构，实际上这个副词也是由形容词转化而来，显然不能按照原文的结构进行翻译，而应转译为两个形容词。例 9 中的 charmingly simple 译成了"美丽单纯"，artlessly fond 译成了"纯朴痴情"；例 10 中的 pinkishly dirty 译成了"脏兮兮的，泛着粉色"。将描述性副词转译成形容词会使译文既生动，又符合中文的表达习惯。

三、英文"形容词+形容词变来的抽象名词"结构的翻译

英文中还有一些结构是"形容词+形容词变来的抽象名词",在句子中作名词应该充当的成分,但实际上由形容词加后缀变来的抽象名词有很强的描述性特征。这种结构如果直接翻译成中文"形容词+名词",会让中文读者感到拗口。比如,bored sullenness 如果译成"厌倦的不快乐"更是让读者摸不着头脑,不如译成"感到厌倦,又闷闷不乐"。同样,bland impudence 译成"淡然的无礼"不如"粗暴无礼,淡然冷漠"更通顺。因此,英文"形容词+形容词变来的抽象名词"结构中形容词变来的抽象名词最好也译成形容词,与前面的形容词同属一种性质。这样会更符合中文的表达习惯。请再看下面的例子。

◆ 例 11

"Oh, I don't care! I don't care what they say!" She whispered, as a *sweet madness* swept over her. (*Gone with the Wind*)

"哎,我不在乎,不在乎他们怎么说,"思嘉嘀咕着,全身充满了<u>甜蜜而又疯狂</u>的感觉。(《飘》)

这个例子中 sweet madness 显然不能译为"甜蜜的疯狂",译成"甜蜜而又疯狂"更符合中文的表达习惯,中文读者更容易接受。

◆ 例 12

They were washed to the sides of the roads, and lay heaped up over the road-gratings, masses of *gorgeous harmonies* in red, brown, and yellow.

它们(落叶)被雨水冲到路的两边,高高地堆在排水口。一堆堆,一丛丛,红、棕、黄交织在一起,<u>绚丽多彩,赏心悦目</u>。

例 12 中如果将 gorgeous harmony 译成"绚丽的和谐",就会令中文读者感到奇怪,不如译成"绚丽多彩,赏心悦目",或至少译成"十分美丽,十分和谐"。

◇ 例 13

She raised an aching head, looked at him with *startled incredulity* and met the pleading eyes of Mammy, who stood behind Gerald's chair. (*Gone with the Wind*)

她抬起痛得要命的头看着他，十分吃惊，满心怀疑。她的视线与嬷嬷恳求的目光相遇，嬷嬷此时正站在嘉乐椅子的后面。(《飘》)

例 13 中的 startled incredulity 如果直接译为"吃惊的猜疑 / 怀疑 / 狐疑"，显然不符合中文的表达习惯，反而将 incredulity 这一由形容词变来的名词转换一下词性，中文就通顺得多。下面例 14 中的原文斜体部分译成译文下划线部分也更为通顺。

◇ 例 14

Will asked calmly and, looking down at him in a confusion of *joy and impotent fury*, Scarlett saw in the quiet depths of his eyes understanding and pity.

威尔平静地问道，思嘉低头看着他，既欣喜若狂，又充满愤怒，同时又无可奈何，她从威尔深邃的眼睛里看到了理解和同情。

拓展练习

翻译下列句子，请注意形容词顺序的调整以及某些副词和抽象名词的翻译。

1. An atmosphere of *refined elegance* pervades the hotel.
2. It also means Chinese competitors such as ZTE and Huawei are replacing *weaker Western* competitors and the list of global competitors.
3. She (Melanie) was not recovering as she should and Scarlett was frightened by her *white weakness*.
4. It wasn't hidebound and stick-in-the-muddish like the older towns and it had a *brash exuberance* that matched her own.
5. Scarlett knew their souls were writhing in *helpless rage* at being under obligations to their Yankee overseer.
6. Its range of sweet specialities includes the famous Bretzeli biscuits, based on a

secret century-old recipe and made from the *purest local* ingredients.

7. They were brief quarrels, short lived because it was impossible to keep a quarrel going with Rhett, who remained *coolly indifferent* to her hot words and waited his chance to pink her in an unguarded spot.

8. It is not a reverent biography: Bartlett admits that Tolstoy was an impossible husband and that he was *unattractively humourless*.

9. The best known is that only an insane airman would be willing to fly such *absurdly dangerous* raids.

10. Herman Hesse, Nobel Prize Winner for Literature, once waxed lyrical about his adopted home town of Ticino: "It's *wonderfully rich and beautiful* and has everything from the Alps to the South".

参考译文与简析

1. 酒店洋溢着<u>精致优雅</u>的气息。(refined elegance 均译成形容词。)

2. 这同时也意味着像中兴和华为这样的中国竞争者正在取代<u>西方较弱的</u>竞争对手以及全球的一些竞争对手。(将两个形容词 weaker 和 Western 在译文中的顺序进行了调整。)

3. 她（梅兰妮）并没有恢复得像正常的那样快，她<u>一脸苍白、瘦弱无比</u>，这让思嘉感到害怕。(white weakness 是形容词 + 形容词变来的抽象名词，译文中译为两个并列形容词，显得更为通顺、自然。)

4. 这座城市并不像一些较老的城镇那样墨守成规，也不落后保守，相反，它<u>有些鲁莽</u>，<u>又生机勃勃</u>，这和思嘉自己的性格正好相似。(brash exuberance 是形容词 + 形容词变来的名词，译文中译成了并列结构。)

5. 思嘉知道，他们因受了北方佬监工的恩惠，<u>心里感到很气愤</u>，<u>却又无可奈何</u>。(helpless rage 是形容词 + 形容词变来的名词，译文中译成了并列结构。)

6. 其中的特色甜品包括著名的金宝丽饼干，这款饼干根据<u>100 多年前的秘密</u>配方制作，全部采用<u>当地最纯</u>的食材。(译文中将 secret 和 century-old、purest 和 local 的顺序根据中文的表达习惯进行了调整。)

7. 这些争吵都是短暂的，持续时间不长，因为不可能和瑞德保持争吵的状态，瑞德对她说出的激烈言辞总是显得沉着冷漠，还会等待时机，冷不防给她一下子。（coolly 和 indifferent 在译文中均译成了形容词，更符合中文的表达习惯。）

8. 这不是一部充满恭敬之辞的传记：巴利特承认，托尔斯泰不适合做丈夫，而且<u>缺乏幽默感，这一点使其毫无魅力可言</u>。（unattractively 是由形容词加后缀变来的副词，意思与 humourless 并列，因此，译文中作并列处理，即"缺乏幽默感，这一点使其毫无魅力可言"。）

9. 大家都知道，只有精神失常的士兵才愿意执行这种<u>既荒谬又危险</u>的空袭任务。（absurdly dangerous 也是副词加形容词的结构，但 absurdly 是由形容词转变而来，意思上与 dangerous 是并列的，所以译文使用并列结构，即"既荒谬又危险"。）

10. 诺贝尔文学奖获得者赫尔曼·黑塞曾这样深情地描述自己的第二故乡提契诺："这里<u>非常富足，又充满魅力</u>，拥有阿尔卑斯山以南的一切。"（wonderfully rich and beautiful 这里译成"非常富足，又充满魅力"。）

第八章　英文名词转译为中文的动词或形容词

总体说来，英文表达倾向静态，中文表达倾向动态。英文的句法成分和词性是对应的，而中文中两者之间没有严格的对应关系。具体说来，英文的动词只能用作谓语，如果表示动词的概念作主语、宾语、定语等，必须改变其形式，这就造成了很多动词加后缀变成名词的现象。而中文比较灵活，动词可以充当非谓语成分，如主语、宾语、定语等，不必改变其形式。英文和中文词性的一个重要差别在于，英文名词占优势，中文动词占优势。两种语言的这种差异使得英译中过程中一些英文的名词需要转译为中文的动词。同时，英文中的一些形容词加后缀变来的名词，翻译时会转换为中文的形容词。

一、英文动词加后缀变来的抽象名词转译为中文的动词

英语中名词用得多，特别是抽象名词，而很多抽象名词又是由动词加后缀变来的，这类词在政论文本和科技文本中使用得尤其频繁。实际上，由动词变来的名词具有很强的动词意义，所以译成中文时，这些名词往往需要还原成动词才能使译文更加通顺。请看下面的例子。

◇ 例 1

The V-Bahn ensures the successful future of tourism for the entire Jungfrau Region in the long term. In this way, we guarantee jobs and an *increase* in added value for the next generations.

从长远看，V 型索道确保了整个少女峰地区旅游业未来取得成功。通过这种方式，能够确保下一代就业，并保证<u>提升</u>其附加值。

◆ 例 2

Bell's decided *opposition* to the scheme, along with that of other friends, kept Helen in Radcliffe and out of what would surely have been a fiasco.

贝尔坚决反对这一计划,加上其他朋友也反对,海伦最终留在了拉德克利夫,避免了一场注定的惨败。

◆ 例 3

Shrewd *use* of resources and a continuous *reduction* in energy use are key pillars of the company's corporate culture.

精细化使用资源和不断减少能源使用是公司企业文化的关键支柱。

◆ 例 4

The higher number of red blood cells then naturally enhances athletes' performance on *return* to the lowlands.

红细胞数量增加自然会使运动员返回低地后取得更好的成绩。

◆ 例 5

Violence against women has been tackled through legislative measures including the new laws on domestic violence and *trafficking* and *exploitation* of women, the *setting up* of new mechanisms for the *protection* and *support* of victims and the *training* of professionals, particularly police officers, involved in the *handling* of violence cases.

针对女性的暴力已通过以下措施解决:首先,立法手段,包括新出台针对家庭暴力及贩运和剥削妇女的法律;其次,建立新机制用来保护和支持受害人;第三,培训参与处理暴力案件的专业人员,尤其是警察。

以上五个例子来自不同文体,包括旅游、传记、科技以及国际组织文献等,其中原文斜体部分均为动词变来的名词,但实际上这些词的动词意义很强,特别是这些词后大多由介词引出其逻辑宾语,因此,翻译时按照中文的表达习惯均转译成动词。特别是例 5 原文中动词加后缀变来的名词特别多,这也是国际组织文献非常重要的特点，翻译时掌握词性转换这一技巧对于译好该类文献具有重要意义，不可忽视。

二、英文动词加 er/or 变来的名词转译为中文动词

英文大部分动词后面都可以加 er 或 or 变成具体名词，表示完成某一动作的人。这类名词有时表示职业，有时只是表示完成这一动作的人，用来说明这个人有一种习惯或专长。如果表示职业，则可以译为"……家"（如"作家""画家"）、"……者"（如"教育工作者""科技工作者"等）、"……手"（如"歌手""水手"）、"……师"（如"教师""摄影师"）、"……员"（如"救生员""教练员"）；如果不表示职业，这类名词最好译成动词。当然，还有些名词不是以 er 或 or 等后缀结尾的名词，翻译时也会根据上下文转译为中文的动词。请看下面的例子。

◇ 例 6

Whether you're in training, a *beginner* or simply *a curious person* trying a new sport, the Crans-Montana trail routes will exceed all your expectations, taking you through exceptional natural surroundings with views that will take your breath away.

无论您在训练，还是仅仅是<u>初学</u>，或者仅仅是<u>出于好奇</u>而尝试一项新运动，克莱恩 - 蒙塔纳的越野路线都将带给您出乎意料的惊喜，带您穿越特殊的自然环境，欣赏令人窒息的美景。

◇ 例 7

More importantly, he was a 20-dollar *tipper*.
更重要的是，他<u>总是给</u>20 美元的<u>小费</u>。

◇ 例 8

Aunt Pitty, who had been a petrified *witness* to the whole scene, suddenly slid to the floor in what was one of the few real fainting spells she had ever had. (*Gone with the Wind*)

白蝶姑妈<u>一直呆呆地看着</u>这一切，突然晕倒在地上。她真正昏厥的时候

不多，但这是其中的一次。(《飘》)

◆ 例 9

Wickramasinghe, at the Cardiff University Centre for Astrobiology in Wales, is Wainwright's *co-author* on the new paper, along with the Indian scientists that sent up the balloon.

威尔士加的夫大学宇宙生物学研究中心的维克勒马辛哈（Wickramasinghe）、温赖特（Wainwright）以及放飞气球的印度科学家<u>共同撰写</u>了这篇新论文。

◆ 例 10

I told Sir Pitt that I was already *A WIFE*.

我告诉皮特爵士我已经<u>结婚了</u>。

以上五个例子中，斜体部分都是名词，即例 6 中的 beginner 和 person、例 7 中的 tipper、例 8 中的 witness、例 9 中的 co-author 以及例 10 中的 wife。虽然词典里这些词均有对应的中文名词，但这里根据上下文和中文的表达习惯译成了动词，显得更为通顺。其中，person 和 wife 实际上永远都只作名词，并非动词转化而来，这里根据上下文也转译成了中文的动词。

三、英文形容词加后缀变来的名词转译为中文形容词

当英文中的形容词在句子中要充当主语、宾语等成分时，需要使用其名词形式，因此这些形容词都可以添加后缀如 -ness、-ity 等变成名词。很多由形容词变来的名词实际上依然是形容词的意思，由于中文表达更倾向于动态，英文句子中由形容词变来的抽象名词译成中文时需要转译为中文的形容词。请看下面的例子。

◆ 例 11

Switzerland is unrivalled when it comes to the *ease*, *comfort* and *variety* of getting around on public transport.

瑞士的公共交通<u>便捷</u>、<u>舒适</u>、<u>多样</u>，无与伦比。

◇ 例 12

Cheese, wine, chocolate, eau de vie, coffee, beer, so many products that illustrate the *richness*, *diversity* and *authenticity* of the beautiful region.

奶酪、葡萄酒、巧克力、白兰地、咖啡、啤酒等产品展示了这一美丽地区<u>丰富多样</u>而又<u>纯正地道</u>的物产。

◇ 例 13

I urged the *cruelty* and *selfishness* of his destroying Mr.s Linton's tranquility for his satisfaction.

我极力跟他说，他为了满足自己的愿望而不惜破坏林顿太太的宁静，那十分<u>残酷</u>和<u>自私</u>。

◇ 例 14

Conservatism, by contrast, lends itself to *wariness*.

与此相反，保守派倾向于<u>谨慎</u>。

◇ 例 15

Small and refined—with the boutique hotels characterized by *personality*, *individuality* and *style*.

精品酒店以"小而精"为原则，<u>独具特色</u>，<u>个性鲜明</u>，<u>雅致时尚</u>。

以上五个例子原文斜体的单词均为形容词变来的抽象名词，翻译成中文时根据中文的表达习惯和特点，译成了中文的形容词，显得十分通顺。

拓展练习

翻译下列句子，请注意英语名词的转译。

1. In the villages and on the plateau of the Jura, *thoroughness, the love of work well-done and ingenuity* are at the root of the know-how used in the precision industry and local gastronomy.

2. According to Helen, Bell unlocked that door with the *suggestion* that Keller write Michael Anagnos, at that time the director of the Perkins Institution.
3. The *targeted protection of habitats of endangered animal species* is just some of the many projects that have been implemented in recent years.
4. Her *engagement* was owing to the remonstrances of Mr. Pitt Crawley, the only *friend* or *protector* Lady Crawley ever had, and the only person, besides her children, for whom she entertained a little feeble *attachment*.
5. Women facing the tragic consequences of *occupation* and subsequent *displacement* have been particularly sensitive on matters of human rights and peace.
6. Bell's *doubts* of his own business acumen led him to decline the suggestion that he administer a trust fund set up for Helen in 1896.
7. His lifelong *commitment* to socialism, combined with the *desire* for cultural communication and democracy, was greatly attractive to a generation of leftists.
8. The increasing *prevalence* of technologies whose effects cross national boundaries has important long-term implications for every country's foreign policy, implications that deserve explicit *recognition* and serious *analysis*.
9. She was essentially a *photographer* of New York and its environs.
10. *Reliability*, *security* and customer *proximity* is included in the philosophy of PostBus Switzerland.

参考译文与简析

1. 汝拉的村庄和高原上，<u>态度严谨、热爱工作以及独出心裁</u>都是精密工业和当地美食技艺的根源。（原文中的名词或名词短语 thoroughness、love of work well-done 和 ingenuity 转译为中文的形容词或名词，即"态度严谨"、"热爱工作"和"独出心裁"。）
2. 海伦表示，贝尔打开了那扇门，<u>建议</u>凯勒写信给当时帕金斯盲人学校的校长迈克尔·阿纳格诺斯。（名词 suggestion 转译为动词"建议"。）
3. 近年来实施了众多项目，包括<u>有针对性地对濒危动物栖息地展开保护</u>等。（名词短语 targeted protection of habitats of endangered animal species 译成了"有针对性地对濒危动物栖息地展开保护"。）

4. 利蓓加能够受聘到这里来全是皮特·克劳利先生力争的结果。全家只有他关心克劳利爵士夫人，并时常保护她。而爵士夫人除了自己的孩子之外，就对他还有点感情。（选自《名利场》，杨必译，有改动）（抽象名词 engagement 和 attachment 转译为动词，具体名词 friend 和 protector 也转译为动词，使得中文表达比较通顺，如果直译为名词会比较拗口。）

5. 面对领土被占、被迫迁移等悲惨结局的妇女对人权和和平问题尤为敏感。（抽象名词 occupation 和 displacement 转译为动词。）

6. 贝尔对自己的商业头脑表示怀疑，这使他拒绝管理 1896 年为海伦设立的信托基金的建议。（名词 doubts 转译为动词。）

7. 他一生致力于社会主义，渴望文化交流与民主，这深深吸引了一代左翼人士。（抽象名词 commitment 和 desire 转译为动词。）

8. 产生国际影响的新技术越来越普遍，对每个国家的外交政策都会产生深远的重要影响，应该明确承认这些影响，并认真分析。（原文中 prevalence、recognition 和 analysis 均转译了词性。）

9. 她基本上在纽约及其周边地区从事摄影工作。或：她基本上拍摄纽约及其周边地区。（photographer 这里不能译成"摄影师"，而应转译为动词。）

10. 瑞士邮政巴士旅游局的服务理念是安全可靠、客户至上。（reliability、security 和 proximity 都是形容词加后缀变来的名词，直译会让人感到拗口，反而转译为形容词。）

第九章　中文动词或形容词译为英文名词

上一章提到，一些英文的名词翻译时需要转译为中文的动词或形容词。那么，中译英时正好相反，中文的一些动词或形容词需要转译为英文的名词，使得译文更符合英文的表达习惯，显得更地道。

一、中文的动词转译为英文名词

中文句子中的动词如果在英译文中不作谓语动词，而是作动词或介词的宾语或者主语，而且该动词的逻辑主语不明显时，一般最好译成英文的名词，即添加以 -ment、-tion、-al 等后缀结尾的抽象名词。请看下面的例子。

◇ 例1

中国正处在工业化、城镇化进程加快，人民收入水平提高和消费结构升级的发展阶段。

China is witnessing the *acceleration* of its industrialization and urbanization, the *increase* of its income and the *upgrading* of its consumption structure.

◇ 例2

自动化要求不断详细了解机器系统的操作，以便一旦有必要就立即采取最佳校正措施。

Automation involves a detailed and continuous *knowledge* of the operation of the machine system, so that the best corrective actions can be taken immediately when necessary.

◇ 例 3

林则徐认为，要成功禁止鸦片买卖，首先就得先将鸦片焚毁。

Lin Zexu believed that a successful *ban* of the trade in opium must be preceded by the *destruction* of the drug itself.

◇ 例 4

一定不要忘记，迄今为止，科学和技术虽然迅猛发展，也不过是未来更迅猛重塑人类环境的前奏。

It must not be forgotten that the rapid *advance* of science and technology until now is but the prelude to even more rapid *remaking* of man's environment in the future.

以上四个例子原文下划线都是动词，但它们在英译文中均不是谓语动词，而是根据上下文译成了名词。这种现象常见于法律文本和科技文本中。请看下面的例子。

◇ 例 5

绝对不允许违反这一原则。

No *violation* of this principle is tolerated.

◇ 例 6

未经甲方书面同意，乙方不得将本协议（包括附件）各项权利及义务全部或者部分转让给第三方。

Without the written *consent* of Party A, the rights and obligations including attachments stipulated herein shall not be completely or partially transferred by Party B to a third party.

以上两个例子来自规定或法律文本，语气比较客观，下划线部分的动词在英译文中作主语或者介词宾语，译成名词更符合英文法律文本的特点。

◇ 例 7

<u>采用</u>这种新装置可以大大降低废品率。

The *adoption* of this new device will greatly cut down the percentage of defective products.

◇ 例 8

显然，地球表面迅速<u>变化</u>，各种废物在大气中<u>扩散</u>，都可能导致天气和气候在不知不觉中发生<u>改变</u>。

The inadvertent *modification* of weather and climate resulting from the rapid *alteration* of the earth's surface and the *dispersion* of wastes of all kinds into the atmosphere is a clear possibility.

以上两个例子中下划线部分的动词在英译文中均充当主语或宾语，语气比较客观，符合科技英语的特点。

中文还有一些动词表示人们的习惯或者特长，翻译时如果译成加 er 或者 or 的具体名词，表示完成该动作的人，更符合英文的表达习惯。请看下面的例子。

◇ 例 9

波士顿的医生对 1100 名 5—9 岁儿童进行了研究，这些儿童的母亲有的<u>吸烟</u>，有的则不吸。

Doctors from Boston studied 1,100 children aged between 5 and 9. Some of their mothers were *smokers* while others were *non-smokers*.

◇ 例 10

孙策<u>性喜打猎</u>，经常在外追赶野兽，他骑的一匹骏马速度极快，侍卫们的马根本追不上。

Sun Ce was a *hunter*, often chasing animals in the wilderness, and the horse he rode ran so fast that his guards' horses could not catch up.

◇ 例 11

他读起书来不分昼夜，废寝忘食。

He was a *voracious reader*, spending much of his days and evenings devouring books.

◇ 例 12

老人直到临终都让他的儿孙们望而生畏。

The old man remained a *terror* to all his descendants to his last day.

以上四个例子原文中下划线部分虽然是动词，但实际上指一种习惯或长期处于某种状态，所以翻译时根据英文的表达习惯转译为名词，这样的译文显得更地道。

二、中文形容词转译为英文名词

上一章提到英文的一些名词翻译成中文时要根据中文的表达习惯转译为中文的形容词，使中译文显得比较跳跃、动态，符合中文读者的预期。由此可见，中文译成英文时，有一些形容词需要根据其在英译文中的成分转译为英文的名词。请看下面的例子。

◇ 例 13

电导率在选择电气材料时很重要。

Electrical conductivity is of *significance* to electrical material selection.

在正式文体中，"……很重要"最好译为 be of significance，这里的"重要"等于转译成了英语的名词。

◇ 例 14

工艺精湛，经久耐用，是我厂产品的主要特点。

Our products are characterized by their *fine workmanship* and *durability*.

这里的"工艺精湛"和"经久耐用"本来是形容词短语，但在英文中作了介词的宾语，所以转译为名词。

◇ 例 15

她对生活很乐观，这让孩子们深受鼓舞。

Her children were inspired by her *optimism* toward life.

这里的"乐观"本来是形容词，但英译文中作了介词的宾语，所以转译为名词。

◇ 例 16

项目实施之前一定要讨论计划是否可行。

The *feasibility* must be discussed before the implementation of the project.

这里"是否可行"中的"可行"是形容词，但因为在译文中需要作 discuss 的宾语，所以变成了名词。另外，由于句子缺乏真正的主语，所以转译过来的名词作句子主语，使用被动语态。

从上文的举例分析可以看出，中文的动词和形容词使用频繁，这是因为中文更重动态和描写，英语则更重视词性与句子成分之间的对应关系。因此，中文的动词和形容词翻译时转译为英文的名词就不奇怪了。

拓展练习

翻译下列句子，请注意中文动词和形容词转译为名词。

1. 神舟十三号载人飞船发射成功，标志着中国在探索宇宙的过程中，又迈出了坚实的脚步。
2. 她虽然不是学音乐的，但非常喜欢音乐，总是购买各种音乐 CD。
3. 禁止任何组织或个人用任何手段侵占或者破坏国家和集体的财产。
4. 实际上，若改进技术和加大捕捞，且不加以控制，只会导致鱼类资源枯竭。

5. 很多家长对孩子们的调皮很焦虑，这实际上对孩子的成长没有好处。
6. 新上任的市长对待普通老百姓很有礼貌，赢得了他们的好感。
7. 只见她脸色苍白，情绪激动，一时说不出话来。
8. 宝玉开悟是由于他意识到与红尘的牵绊都是自己造成的。
9. 要不是我特别擅长做精细活，早就被辞退了。
10. 天快黑了，要考虑你一个人去那个偏远的地方是否安全。

参考译文与简析

1. *The success of the launching* of the crewed spacecraft Shenzhou XIII marked a solid step in China's progress of space exploration.（原文中的副词"成功"和动词"发射"的词性在译文中发生了变化，均译成了名词 success 和 launching。）

2. She is not a *major* in music, but a *lover* of it and a *buyer* of music CDs.（"学音乐""喜欢音乐"和"购买各种音乐CD"均译成了英语名词 major、lover 和 buyer。）

3. *Appropriation* or *damaging* of state or collective property by any organization or individual by whatever means is prohibited.（根据英语的表达习惯，动词"侵占"和"破坏"转译为英语名词 appropriation 和 damaging。）

4. In fact, *improved technology* and *greater fishing effort*, uncontrolled, would lead only to *depletion* of fish *resources*.（动宾短语"改进技术"和"加大捕捞"以及主谓短语"资源枯竭"转译为英语名词短语 improved technology、greater fishing effort 和 depletion。）

5. Many parents' *anxiety* about their children's naughtiness is harmful to the latter's growth.（中文形容词"焦虑"转译为英语名词 anxiety。）

6. The new mayor earned appreciation of the common people through his *courtesy* to them.（中文形容词"很有礼貌"转译为英语名词 courtesy。）

7. The *pallor* of her face indicated her *rage*, which caused her *speechlessness* at the moment.（中文形容词"苍白""激动"和动词"说不出话来"均转译为英语名词 pallor、rage 和 speechlessness。）

8. Baoyu's *enlightenment* is brought on by his *realization* that his bonds to the Red Dust are of his own *creation*.（动词"开悟""意识到"和"造成"均转译为英语名词，

即 enlightenment、realization 和 creation。）

9. But for my *proficiency* in doing fine work, I would have been dismissed.（中文动词"擅长"译为英语名词 proficiency。）

10. It is getting dark, so you have to consider the *safety* of going alone to the remote area.（中文形容词"安全"译为英语名词 safety。）

第十章　英文被动语态的翻译

被动语态是英文中一种常见的语法现象，其使用范围之广、频率之高都是中文无法比拟的，特别是英文的信息类文体（如科技文体、新闻文体、公文及论说性文体等），被动语态可以说比比皆是，因为在这类文体中使用被动语态，会显得客观、翔实、公正、正式，避免给人以主观臆断、啰唆冗长的感觉。当然，英文其他文体也会使用被动语态。中文被动语态使用比较少，而且表示被动意义的"被""挨""遭""受""给""叫""让""为""为/被……所"等大部分字眼都有"遭受"之意，对于动作的承受者来说，大多是其不盼望发生的事情。因此，除少数情况外，英文译成中文时被动语态大多数会变成主动语态。

一、英文被动语态译为中文被动语态

如上文所述，如果英文的被动语态对于动作的承受者来说是其不盼望或不企及的事情，英文的被动语态则可以译为中文的被动语态。请看下面的例子。

◆ 例 1

The murderer *was caught* yesterday, and it is said that he will *be hanged*.
凶手已于昨日被捕，据说他将被绞死。

◆ 例 2

He says he *was kidnapped* when he was two, but managed to escape four years later.
他说自己两岁时遭到绑架，但四年后设法逃了出来。

◇ 例 3

Probably no more than a few hundred thousand Africans *were taken* to the Americas before 1600.

1600 年之前，约有几十万的非洲人被运到美洲大陆。

◇ 例 4

During the early years of the transatlantic slave trade, the Portuguese generally purchased Africans who *had been captured* and enslaved during tribal wars.

早期跨大西洋奴隶贸易中，葡萄牙人通常购买部落战争中被俘虏并成为奴隶的非洲人。

以上四个例子中，原文下划线部分均为被动语态，对于动作的承受者来说，hang、kidnap、take 和 capture 都是不好的事情，可以译为中文的被动语态。

二、英语被动语态译为中文主动语态

（一）译为"受事者＋动词"结构

如果英文使用被动语态的句子中没有 by 引出动作的发出者，或者没有用来修饰整句话的时间状语或地点状语，这样的句子一般先按照原文的顺序翻译，省译"被"字，然后检查中文的句子是否通顺即可，毕竟中文里有很多句子就是这种意义被动、形式主动的句子。请看下面的例子。

◇ 例 5

Technological developments *cannot be predicted* in detail, but neither are they impenetrable.

技术发展的方方面面不可能详细预测，但也并非不可实现。

◇ 例 6

Hiltl, the first vegetarian restaurant in the world, *was founded* in 1898 in Zurich and still remains a firm favourite today.

希尔特尔是全球第一家素食餐厅，1898 年创建于苏黎世，至今仍深受喜爱。

◇ 例 7

A replacement for the ineffective League of Nations, the organization *was created* following the Second World War to prevent another such conflict.

其前身为国际联盟，二战后为防止类似冲突再次发生而成立。

◇ 例 8

But even as the great and the near great gravitated to her small parlor, so unfortunates found their way to her cellar where they *were fed, bedded and sent* on their way with packages of food. (*Gone with the Wind*)

就像重要的人和几近重要的人被吸引到梅兰妮的客厅一样，这些不幸的人来到她的地下室，在那里，他们有饭吃，有床睡，继续上路时还带上一包包食物。(《飘》)

以上英文原句均译为中文形式上的主动句，但原文的主谓顺序没有改变。如果上述中译文添加"被"字，势必会显得拗口，不符合中文的语感。但有的英文被动语态译成中文时语序不变，需要译成"是……的"结构。

◇ 例 9

The march could not *be stopped* by bullets now.

现在，游行已经不是子弹所能阻止的了。

◇ 例 10

Poets *are born*, but orators *are made*.

诗人是天生的，演说家是后天造就的。

（二）译为"施事者＋动词"结构

如果原文以某种方式说出了具体的实施者，尤其是以 by 引出了动作的发出者，则根据中文句子的特点，可以将原文译为"具体施事者＋动词"结构。请看下面的例子。

◇ 例 11

What measures *have been or are being adopted by the local government* to reduce air pollution?

<u>当地政府已经采取何种措施或正在采取何种措施</u>以减少空气污染？

◇ 例 12

Their liberty *will be inviolably protected by Time as well as Space*.

<u>时间和空间将保护</u>这些星际殖民地，使其自由不受侵犯。

◇ 例 13

He has been pursued, day by day, and year by year, *by a most phenomenal and astonishing luckiness*.

一天天，一年年，<u>幸运总是伴随他，令人惊诧不已</u>。（或：一天天，一年年，<u>他始终吉星高照，令人惊诧不已</u>。）

上述几个例子中，每个句子原文都由 by 引出了动作的发出者，即施事者，所以不妨将这一"施事者"提前，变成中文真正意义上的主动语态。

如果原句中没有出现具体的施事者，但根据上下文可以推断其施事者是泛指的人，此时，中译文可以用"人们""有人""大家"或"我们"等泛指名词作主语，也就是说译成"泛指主语＋动词"的格式，特别是当原句中的谓语动词表示人的感觉、意识、思想、看法、观点、感知等时，如 see、hear、observe、taste、feel、find/discover、think、believe、know、doubt 等。请看下面的例子。

◇ 例 14

The health-promoting climate of Davos' mountain air *was discovered* as far back as 1853.

早在 1853 年，<u>人们就发现</u>达沃斯山区的空气有益健康。

◇ 例 15

Although *little is known* about how hypnosis works, it has been made use of in medical treatment.

虽然人们对催眠术知之甚少，但该技术已用于临床治疗。

◇ 例 16

It *is believed* that they were extraterrestrial or hollow earth children.

人们认为，他们是天外来客或地心孩子。

◇ 例 17

The big man *was seen* running away from the scene of the crime, with something black under his arm.

有人看见那个高个子男人从犯罪现场跑开了，胳膊下面夹着一个黑色的东西。

例 14—17 原文中的动词 discover、know、believe、see 都与人的感知和观点相关，翻译时将被动语态转换成以泛指代词"人们""有人"等为主语的主动语态，显然更符合中文的表达习惯。至于泛指主语是"人们""大家"还是"有人"，要根据上下文确定。

（三）译成无主句或者"话题－评述"句

英文被动语态的动词如果表示建议、命令、请求、要求等，特别是原句有 should、must、has to、shall 等情态动词，或者有 suggest、require、need、request、ask 等表示建议、要求、请求的动词，且句子中也没有由 by 引出的动作发出者时，可以考虑译成无主句。如果句子中有时间或地点状语修饰全句，则可以将时间或地点放在前面作话题，译成"话题－评述"句。

◇ 例 18

No money *shall be drawn from the treasury* but in consequence of appropriations made by law; and a regular statement and account of the receipts and expenditures of all public money shall be published from time to time.

除法律规定外，<u>不得从国库中提取任何款项</u>；一切公款收支的报告和账目应经常公布。

◇ 例 19

A modest prediction *may be made* that in the future there will be many more challenges to the continued public support of science, especially expensive fields of science, when the beneficial results are not obvious and the potentially harmful effects, though unknown in detail, are feared.

<u>可以做一个适度的预测</u>：未来，如果科学带来的益处并不明显，而潜在的有害影响虽然不详，却令人担心，那么公众对科学的持续支持将会面临更多挑战，特别是费用昂贵的科学领域。

◇ 例 20

Studies over time *are required* to test the extent to which recommendations have been accepted, put into practice and had an impact.

<u>需要</u>一段时间的研究来考查接受和实施建议并发挥其影响的情况。

◇ 例 21

But it *must be realized* that, even now, the resources required for such a project may not be beyond the capabilities of a single large state (a Bering Straits dam—one method—is entirely feasible at costs comparable to large continental dams).

但是，<u>必须认识到</u>，即使是现在，这样一个项目所需的资源可能不会超出一个大国的能力（其中一种方法是建造白令海峡大坝，其成本与在大陆修建大坝相当，完全可行）。

以上四个例子原文中的被动语态要么有情态动词，要么动词是 require，句子中也没有时间或地点状语需要在翻译时提至前面，因此译成中文的无主句比较通顺，而且符合中文的表达习惯。英文的被动语态如果是 it is reported / said，一般都译成"据报道"或"据说",实际上也是一种无主句。

◇ 例 22

In 2016, for example, a Lunchtime Cinema *was organized* to raise employee awareness on the subject of food waste.

2016 年举办了"午餐电影院"活动,以提高员工对食物浪费问题的认识。

◇ 例 23

In addition to the survey, sub-regional consultative workshops *are being held*, for example in Uganda and Mali.

除调查工作,乌干达和马里等国家还在举办分区咨询研讨会。

◇ 例 24

In a next construction stage, the balconies, the outer facade and the driveway to the hotel *will be renovated*. Moreover, the entire reception area will be given a facelift and be totally redesigned.

下一阶段将对宾馆的阳台、外立面和通往宾馆的车道进行改建。此外,整个接待区也进行了重新设计,使该区域的面貌焕然一新。

◇ 例 25

The Tell Pass *can be purchased* at the Tourist Information in Lucerne's railway station where a team are on hand every day to provide you with professional advice.

卢塞恩火车站的游客信息中心可以购买泰尔通票,该中心还有一个团队每天为游客提供专业建议。

◇ 例 26

Soon, in the heart of the Swiss Riviera, an astonishing museum dedicated to the life and times of Charlie Chaplin *will be unveiled*.

不久,瑞士里维埃拉的中心地带将出现一座令人震撼的博物馆,专门展示查理·卓别林的生平。

例22—26原文中均有地点或时间状语，且没有关于施事者的任何信息，翻译成中文时时间或地点状语均省译了介词，将时间或地点名词放在了句首，成为话题–评述结构，而且原文的被动语态转化成了主动语态，符合中文表达习惯。

（四）译成"把"字句或使动句

中文还有一种结构叫"把"字句或使动句，主要表示对人或物如何"处置"，所以也叫"处置句"。如果英文被动句的主干暗示一种结果，可以根据情况译成"把"字句或使动句，此时原句中的主语就放在"把"字的后面，如果原文的文体比较正式，可以将"把"字改为"将"字。请看下面的例子。

◆ 例 27

By evening the occupation was complete and the people *were chased off* the streets by an eight o'clock curfew.

到傍晚的时候，占领结束，八点开始的宵禁把人们从街道赶走。

◆ 例 28

Metals *are deliberately mixed* to produce hundreds of new substances with desirable qualities not otherwise available.

有意识地将各种金属混合在一起，可以产生数百种新物质。这些物质的特性合乎人们的需要，也是一般金属所没有的。

以上两个例句的被动语态均强调结果，所以将它们译成中文的"处置句"，第一句译为"把"字句，而第二句由于原文属于科技文体，比较正式，没有使用"把"字，而使用"将"字，更符合原文的语气。

另外，有施事者或暗含原因的英文被动句也可以根据情况译成中文的使动句，原句中的主语放在"使"字的后面。

◇ 例 29

Sometimes a rock *is made* into a very strange shape because softer parts are worn away and harder parts are left.

有时，由于岩石较松软的部分剥落，较坚硬的部分保留，使岩石呈现出奇形怪状。

◇ 例 30

The big trees *were rooted up* by the heavy storm last night.

昨晚的一场暴风雨使得这些大树连根拔起。

例 29 的原句后半部分是前面被动部分的原因，所以将原因先译出，后面使用使动句，使句子通顺流畅。当然，后半部分也可以不使用"使"字，直接使用表示结果的分句，整个句子译成：有时，由于岩石较松软的部分剥落，较坚硬的部分保留，岩石便呈现出奇形怪状。这个译文中最后添加了一个"便"字，译文通顺，逻辑关系清楚明了。例 30 后半部分用 by 引出了动作的发出者，译文将动作的发出者作为主语，后面用了使动用法，译文读起来也比较通顺。

拓展练习

请注意英语被动语态的翻译。

1. There are around 100 different kinds of vegetables *farmed* in Switzerland that *are delivered* fresh to restaurants.
2. Every Wednesday and Saturday morning, the 50 or so stalls of the "Soledurner Märet" *are set up* on the winding streets of the delightful old town. Solothurn *is known as* Switzerland's finest baroque city, while its weekly market *is described* as one of the prettiest and liveliest in the country.
3. Space can *be mapped and crossed and occupied* without definable limit; but it can never *be conquered*.
4. Also the entire F&B area with the lounge and the half board restaurant will *be restructured and refurbished*.

5. The appliance *is equipped with* a replacement reminder which reminds you to replace the shaving heads.
6. The ancient Chinese sages said that illness and disease should first *be treated* with diet, then acupuncture and then Chinese herbs.
7. Both natural vegetation and crops *are affected* by acid rain. The roots *are damaged* by acidic rainfall, causing the growth of the plant to *be stunted*, or even in its death.
8. If an asteroid or comet is large enough, microbes could *be frozen* deep within.
9. Transtromer has long *been recognized* as the most influential Scandinavian poet of the post-World War II era. His work has *been translated* into more than 50 languages.
10. In addition, reports concerning investigation of each individual complaint, *are submitted* to the competent public service department/officer, and contain, in the event of the finding of violation, the Ombudsman's suggestions or recommendations for reparation measures within specified period.

参考译文与简析

1. 瑞士种植大约100种蔬菜，可新鲜送达餐厅。（英文中的两处被动语态均转译为中文的主动语态。）
2. 每个星期三和星期六早上，索洛图恩集市的50多个"Soledurner Märet"摊位就会出现在迷人的老城蜿蜒的街道上。人们称索洛图恩为瑞士最迷人的巴洛克风格城市，其每周集市也是瑞士最美、最热闹的集市。（英文句子中的被动语态均转译为中文的主动语态，前面一句中被动语态译为"……出现在"，后一句中添加了"人们"作主语。）
3. 人类可以为太空绘图，可以穿越太空和占领太空，没有任何限制；但人类永远无法征服太空。（原文分号前后均使用被动语态，中译文均转译为主动语态，添加"人们"作主语。）
4. 除此之外，整个F&B区域（含休息室）以及半膳餐馆也将进行改建和重新装饰。（原文的被动语态转译为中文的主动语态，原文的顺序没有改变，直接省译"被"字。）
5. 本电器配有更换提示，会提醒您更换剃须刀头。（原文的被动语态转译为中文的主动语态,直接省译"被"字,语序没有改变。)

6. 中国古代圣人认为,疾病应该首先通过饮食进行治疗,其次是针灸,再其次是草药。(原文的被动语态转译为中文的主动语态,直接省译"被"字,语序没有改变。)

7. 自然植被和庄稼都受到酸雨的影响,其根部遭到酸雨破坏,使得植物的生长受到阻碍,甚至引起植物死亡。(原文的被动语态基本上保留,中文中"受""遭"等都是被动语态的标识。)

8. 如果小行星或彗星足够大,就可以将微生物冷冻在内部。(原文的被动语态直接译成主动语态。)

9. 特朗斯特罗姆长期以来被公认为二战之后斯堪的纳维亚半岛最具影响力的诗人,其作品已译成50多种语言。(原文中有两个被动语态 has long been recognized 和 has been translated,前者直接译为被动语态,后者译为"已译成",直接省略"被"字,成为主动语态。)

10. 另外,关于每个投诉的调查报告均提交给职能公共服务部门/官员,里面含监察员的建议,即若发现侵犯人权的情况,在一定时间内需采取何种弥补措施。(原文的被动语态转译为主动语态,语序没有发生改变。)

第十一章　英文"形容词+名词"和中文"名词+形容词"互换

我们在学习英语和翻译的过程中会注意到这样一种现象，即当描述人、事、物或地点时，英文倾向使用"形容词+名词"的结构，即中心落在名词上，体现出英文静态的特点。如"树很高"或"雨很大"在比较正式的英语中通常会写成 It is a tall tree 或 It is a heavy rain，而非 The tree is tall 或 The rain is heavy，当然后面的说法在英语口语中也会使用。中文则正好相反，当描述人、事、物或地点时，更倾向使用"名词+形容词"的结构，即中心落在形容词上，突出汉语的动态特点。英文和中文的这一差别说明，翻译时需要进行相关转换，即英语"形容词+名词"结构和中文"名词+形容词"结构通常需要互相转换。下面分别举例说明。

一、英文"形容词+名词"结构转译为中文"名词+形容词"结构

如上文所述，英文中描述人或事物时一般使用"形容词+名词"结构，特别在书面表达中更是如此。该结构如果直译出来，中文会显得比较静态，句子往往不够通顺。因此，最好转译为中文的"名词+形容词"结构。请看下面的例子。

◇ 例 1

When our race has reached its *ultimate achievements*, and the stars themselves are scattered no more widely than the seed of Adam, even then we shall still be like ants crawling on the face of the earth.

即使我们的成就登峰造极，我们可以遍布每个星球，我们依然就像地球表面爬行的蚂蚁一样。

◇ 例 2

The *cold, dark climate*, where doors are bolted and curtains drawn, provides a perfect setting for crime writing.

<u>天气阴冷</u>，房门紧锁，窗帘密掩，一切为犯罪小说写作提供了完美的背景。

◇ 例 3

The first team of horses was led by a *hale, ruddy-faced old man*, between seventy and eighty, whom I have known for years.

第一队马由一位<u>老人</u>领着，我已认识老人多年。他七八十岁，<u>面色红润</u>，<u>精神矍铄</u>。

◇ 例 4

Hippolita, his wife, an *amiable lady*, did sometimes venture to represent the danger of marrying their only son so early, considering his *great youth*, and *greater infirmities*; but she never received any other answer than reflections on her own sterility, who had given him but one heir.

公爵夫人希珀丽塔<u>温柔善良</u>，有时却敢大胆地表白她的忧虑：他们唯一的儿子还<u>太小</u>，更何况他身体现在<u>这么虚弱</u>，不该这么早结婚。可是，得到的回答却总是让她反思自己的生育能力，因为公爵夫人只为公爵生了一个儿子。

以上例子均出自文学作品，斜体部分都是"形容词＋名词"的形式，中译文均将名词提到了形容词的前面，显得句子描写性更强，更加动态，符合中文的表达习惯和思维习惯。这类转化在旅游文本中更为常见。请看下面的例子。

◇ 例 5

And just like it started—with *sunny days and breathtaking views*—the winter season is now definitely coming to an end here in the Matterhorn ski paradise.

一如既往，这里<u>阳光依然明媚</u>，<u>景色依然令人叹为观止</u>，马特洪峰滑雪天堂的冬季即将结束。

◇ 例 6

The Glacier Express is superb in all four seasons: *shimmering peaks* in summer, *snow-covered, fairy-tale scenery* in winter, *fabulous Alpine flowers* in spring and a *kaleidoscope of colour* in autumn.

冰川快车一年四季均非比寻常：春季，阿尔卑斯山花娇艳动人；夏季，巍峨的山峰熠熠生辉；秋季，色彩一片斑斓，仿佛万花筒；冬季，白雪皑皑，宛如童话仙境。

◇ 例 7

It offers a *charming landscape* of fertile plains and wooded hills.

这里肥沃的平原和树木繁茂的山丘景色宜人。

◇ 例 8

Blue-green lakes, picturesque chalet villages and *eternally white mountain summits*—this is where you will experience picturesque Switzerland!

这里碧蓝的湖泊波光粼粼，木屋村庄风景如画，巍峨的山峰终年白雪皑皑——您将体验到如诗如画的瑞士！

以上四个例子的原文均出自旅游文本，斜体部分基本使用了"形容词 + 名词"的结构，翻译成中文时这些结构转换成了"名词 + 形容词"结构，符合中文的表达习惯和审美预期，可以更好地起到旅游宣传的效果。

二、中文"名词 + 形容词"结构转译为英语"形容词 + 名词"结构

与前文的英译中相反，中文的一些"名词 + 形容词"结构在译为英文时，需要根据英文的表达习惯将形容词提前，将名词后置，即转译为英文"形容词 + 名词"的结构。请看下面的例子。

◇ 例 9

袁绍为人宽厚文雅，有气度，喜怒不形于色，但性格刚愎自用，难于采

纳别人的正确意见，所以最终失败。

Yuan Shao was *a generous and elegant man*, never showing his joy or anger, but he was *such a headstrong man* that he seldom adopted others' advice, and as a result, he ultimately failed.

◇ 例 10

东家的柳树矮一点儿，不必向路人解释本来有长高的可能；西家的槐树高一点儿，也不必向邻居说明自己并没有独占风水的企图。

He who has *a short willow tree* does not necessarily explain to the passers-by that it could have grown taller, nor does he who has *a tall Chinese scholar tree* necessarily explain that he has had no intention to occupy a favourable piece of land.

◇ 例 11

正是因为上学的缘故，也是因为山桃儿渐渐长大的缘故，她对世界的疑问也就越来越多了。

Because of her attending school and growing up, Shantao had *more and more questions* about the world.

以上三个例子原文下划线部分均是名词放在前面，形容词放在后面，显示出中文的动态特征。翻译时，根据英文的表达习惯进行了调整，将形容词放在了名词的前面。

中文旅游文本中"名词+形容词"结构使用比较频繁，翻译时要注意转换成英文的"形容词+名词"结构。请看下面的例子。

◇ 例 12

西藏地势高，气候较寒冷，昼夜温差大，但由于日照时间长，冬季并不十分冷。

At *a high altitude*, Tibet has *a cold climate* and *a big temperature difference between day and night*, but thanks to *the long sunshine duration*, it has *a mild winter*.

这个例子非常典型，基本每个小分句都是"名词+形容词"结构，翻译时这些结构均转译为"形容词+名词"结构，即译文中的斜体部分。

◇ 例 13

交通便利，环境优美，富有娱乐性、惊险性和刺激性的锦江游乐园各种项目深受游客欢迎。

With *easy access*, *sound environment* and exciting facilities for an adrenaline rush, Jinjiang Amusement Park appeals to tourists.

◇ 例 14

景区内河流密布、森林茂密、野生动物、植物繁多，原始生态环境保存完好，金丝大峡谷是休闲度假、寻觅探幽的旅游胜地。

Renowned for *rivers, lush forests, various wild animals and plant species* and hence the well-preserved ecological system, the Jinsi Grand Canyon is a superb tourist attraction for recreation and sightseeing.

◇ 例 15

城内古街古巷曲径通幽，石桥城垣错落有致，碧水晨雾姿态万千，春江渔火诗意盎然，有雄伟奇特、蜚声中外的国家级重点文物保护单位青龙洞古建筑群和明清古民居、古巷道、古码头、古城垣等160余处，观赏价值与科考价值俱高。

The Old Town is of *great aesthetic and scientific value*, with *winding paths*, *stone bridges*, *clear waters veiled in mist*, and *boats on rivers*. There are more than 160 famous spectacular national relic sites, such as the Qinglong Cave Building Complex, traditional houses, alleys, docks, and the old city walls.

例 13–15 的原文均来自中文旅游文本，下划线部分均侧重描写，采用了"名词+形容词"结构，符合中文的表达习惯和审美预期，翻译时根据英文描写人或物的习惯，将形容词或其他修饰词作定语，名词放在中心位置。

通过上述举例分析，翻译学习者需要了解中英文在描写人或物时的表达习惯，并根据两种语言的不同进行一定的转换，这样才能保证译文符合目的语的表达习惯，才能使译文更加地道，否则中译文会显得欧化，英译文有"中式英语"的感觉。

拓展练习

翻译下列句子，请注意英文"形容词+名词"结构和中文"名词+形容词"结构互换。

1. More magnificent horses never were seen; *glossy coats*, *tremendous haunches*, strong enough to shake a house if it came to an earnest pull, *immense feet*, *slow-stepping*: very gentle the huge creatures seemed.

2. The canton of Vaud offers *multiple gastronomic facets*: from fine restaurants rated in the world-renowned gastronomic guides to the vast variety of terroir specialties.

3. The region, a true miniature Switzerland, with its *breathtaking*, *varied landscapes* ranging from Alpine peaks to the shores of Lake Geneva, is a delight for visitors.

4. Orbiting communications relays will grow substantially in channel capacity, and are likely to be increasingly sophisticated, with *well-defined geographical coverage*, *increased power*, *and specialized capabilities*.

5. The "Classic" tour offers something of everything: *picturesque towns*, *breathtaking train rides*, *thrilling mountain excursions*.

6. 天津大剧院总建筑面积10.5万平方米，建筑设计意为"城市舞台"，建筑形式简洁大气，和谐圆润。

7. 南澳岛是广东省唯一海岛县，岛上风光旖旎，景色秀美，最迷人之处是青澳湾。

8. 度假区内的海域海水纯净，陆岸植被丰富，环境优雅宁静，空气格外清新，可容纳国际上最大规模的沙滩运动娱乐项目和海上运动娱乐项目，是中国南方最理想的滨海浴场和海上运动场所。

9. 云冈石窟依山而凿，东西绵延约一公里，气势恢宏，内容丰富，是中国最大的石窟之一，与敦煌莫高窟、洛阳龙门石窟和麦积山石窟并称为中国四大石窟艺术宝库。

10. 现存主要洞窟 45 个，造像 59000 余尊，最高的 17 米，最小的仅有几厘米，各类造像<u>形象生动活泼</u>，<u>姿态飘逸隽秀</u>。

参考译文与简析

1. 从来没有见过这么威武的马儿：<u>毛皮光滑</u>；<u>后腿健硕</u>，壮得只要用力一拉便可撼动一座房子；<u>马蹄巨大无比</u>，<u>脚步缓慢</u>。这些高大的马匹又似乎非常温顺。（原文中有几个"形容词 + 名词"结构的短语，包括 glossy coats、tremendous haunches、immense feet 和 slow-stepping，这些短语均转译为中文"名词 + 形容词"的结构，即"毛皮光滑""后腿健硕""马蹄巨大无比"和"脚步缓慢"。）

2. 沃州的<u>美食丰富多彩</u>：从世界著名美食指南中的高分餐厅到种类繁多的当地特色美食，应有尽有。（原文中"形容词 + 名词"结构的短语 multiple gastronomic facets 译为"美食丰富多彩"，很显然，名词放在前面，形容词后置，更符合中文的表达习惯。）

3. 该地区堪称真正的微缩版瑞士，从阿尔卑斯山峰到日内瓦湖岸，<u>多种美景令人叹为观止</u>，<u>赏心悦目</u>。（原文中 breathtaking, varied landscapes 是"形容词 + 名词"结构，译文中将名词前置，即"多种美景令人叹为观止，赏心悦目"，读起来更为通顺。）

4. 在轨通信中继卫星的信道容量将大大增加，而且可能变得越来越复杂，<u>地理覆盖范围划定明确</u>，<u>功率提高</u>，<u>能力进一步专业化</u>。（原文三个"形容词 + 名词"结构的短语均转译为了中文"名词 + 动词"结构。）

5. 这段旅程中，经典景点令人应接不暇：<u>城镇风景如画</u>，<u>火车游览令人叹为观止</u>，<u>高山游览惊险刺激</u>。（原文 picturesque towns, breathtaking train rides, thrilling mountain excursions 转译为"城镇风景如画，火车游览令人叹为观止，高山游览惊险刺激"，语序调整后中文读起来很通顺，符合表达习惯。）

6. Tianjin Grand Theater covers a floor area of 105,000 square meters. The design of the theater derives from the concept of "City Stage", featuring *simple structure and grand ambiance*.（原文中"建筑形式简洁大气，和谐圆润"属于"名词 + 形容词"的结构，转译为英文的"形容词 + 名词"结构，即 simple structure and grand ambiance。）

7. Nan'ao Island is the only island county in Guangdong Province, boasting *stunning*

scenery, with Qing'ao Bay as the most charming site. (原文的"风光旖旎,景色秀美"两个短语都是"名词 + 形容词"结构,且意思相近,符合中文描写特征,译文中转译为"形容词 + 名词"结构,即 stunning scenery。)

8. With *clear water, lush vegetation along the coast, fresh air and peaceful environment*, it is the best beach for seaside bathing and marine sports in the south of China, and it can hold the world's largest-scale beach and marine sports activities. (原文中"海水纯净,陆岸植被丰富,环境优雅宁静,空气格外清新"这一部分均为"名词 + 形容词"结构,译文中均转译为"形容词 + 名词"结构,有的顺序还进行了调整,符合英语的表达习惯。)

9. Carved into the cliffs at the mountains, the *grand* Yungang Grottoes, which stretch about one kilometer from east to west, constitute one of the largest grottoes in China. The scenic spot is known as one of the four famous grotto art treasures in the country, the other three being the Dunhuang Mogao Caves, Luoyang Longmen Grottoes and Maiji Mountain Grottoes. ("气势恢宏,内容丰富"在译文中简化处理,将 grand 一词放在名词的前面。)

10. There are 45 major caves and around 59,000 statues with *vivid images and postures*, the biggest being 17 meters tall and the smallest only several centimeters tall. (原文侧重描写的部分"形象生动活泼,姿态飘逸隽秀"是"名词 + 形容词"结构,译文中简化处理,且将形容词放在了名词前面,符合英语的表达习惯,即 vivid images and postures。)

第十二章　英译中名词的重复和中译英名词的省译

英文中经常出现这样的现象，即两个形容词或其他形式的定语修饰一个名词，或两个动词后面加一个宾语，这种表达比较简洁，符合英语不重复同一名词的特点。但译成中文时，如果按照原文翻译，有时句子会显得不通顺，或者翻译不到位，这时若将名词重复翻译，反而会使译文通顺。中文中如果不同的定语修饰一个名词，或者不同的动词后面加的是同一名词，这个名词往往重复。因此，中译英时，重复的名词一般要作省译处理。下面通过举例说明此类名词的重复和省译。

一、英文不同定语或动词之后名词的重复翻译

在翻译实践中经常会遇到英文不同定语修饰同一名词的现象，如果按照原文结构进行翻译，中译文往往不够通顺，表达没有力度，如果翻译时将名词重复一下，中译文则更显通顺地道。比如，The perfect infrastructure for private and business events 译成"完善的基础设施适合举办各种私人和商务活动"，显然不如"完善的基础设施适合举办各种私人活动和商务活动"通顺。原文中的 private 和 business 均修饰 events，翻译时将 events 重复翻译更符合中文的表达习惯。再比如，create and consume data 译成"创造和使用数据"不如译成"创造数据和使用数据"。下面请看更多的例子。

◇ 例1

With around 350 *intercity and interurban train* connections daily, Zurich Airport is a key hub in the Swiss rail network. International, regional and local public transport companies converge at Zurich Airport, making it easy to reach.

每天大约 350 趟城际铁路列车和市际列车使苏黎世机场成为瑞士铁路网的一个核心枢纽。国际、地区和当地公共交通公司齐聚苏黎世机场，使这里的交通极为便利。

◇ 例 2

Today, most of the smaller countries of the world are unable to utilize *all or even many modern technologies* because of their limited national resources.

如今，由于国家资源有限，全世界大多数小国都无法利用<u>全部现代技术或大多现代技术</u>。

◇ 例 3

Passengers are offered a wide range of catering options such as *regional, national and international specialities*—whether on board a historic paddle steamer, along the country's most beautiful train routes or during shopping stopovers at RailCity stations.

无论是乘坐历史悠久的明轮船、乘坐火车飞奔在瑞士最美丽的铁路线上，还是在火车站购物中心（RailCity）购物，游客都可品尝到种类繁多的<u>地区特色美食、瑞士特色美食及外国 / 异域特色美食</u>。

以上三个例子原文中均有两个或两个以上的形容词修饰一个名词的情况，翻译时重复这一名词更符合中文的表达习惯。如例 3 的译文"地区特色美食、瑞士特色美食及外国 / 异域特色美食"显然比"地区、瑞士及国际特色美食"要更通顺。

◇ 例 4

Among the most outstanding achievements was the completion in 1882 of the 15-kilometre Gotthard Train Tunnel through the Alps, opening up unprecedented *potential for travel and transportation* on the important north-south-north route.

其中最杰出的成就之一是 1882 年竣工的圣哥达铁路隧道。这一隧道穿越阿尔卑斯山，长达 15 公里，激发出重要的北 - 南 - 北线路上空前的旅行<u>潜力</u>和交通<u>潜力</u>。

◆ 例 5

Another is *the potentially poisonous effects on plants and fish and ultimately on man* of increased spread of pesticides and herbicides.

另一个例子是，杀虫剂和除草剂适用范围扩大，会对植物和鱼类产生潜在的毒性作用，并最终也会对人类产生潜在的毒性作用。

以上两个例子中，例 4 中 potential 后面跟了两个介词短语作后置定语，翻译时，后置定语提到名词"潜力"的前面，这时重复一下名词"潜力"，中文会显得更加通顺。potential for travel and transportation 译成"旅行潜力和交通潜力"显然比"旅行和交通潜力"更通顺。例 5 中 effects on plants and fish and ultimately on man 译成"对植物和鱼类产生潜在的毒性作用，并最终也会对人类产生潜在的毒性作用"比译成"对植物和鱼类并最终对人类产生潜在的毒性作用"更通顺，意思也更清晰。

◆ 例 6

Might it be useful, therefore, to begin to support some sciences—or perhaps all—through *international as well as national mechanisms*?

开始使用国际机制和国家机制支持一些学科（也许是所有学科）是否有益？

这个例子的两个形容词 international 和 national 后面跟了一个名词 mechanisms，翻译时将这一名词重复，更符合中文的习惯。否则，译成"国际和国家机制"显然不通顺，而且意思也不清晰。

二、中文不同定语或动词后面重复的名词省译

中译英时，为使译文更符合目的语习惯，常常需要省译相邻重复的名词。比如"观察自然、描述自然"译为 observe and describe nature，而非 observe nature and describe nature。请看下面更多的例子。

◇ 例 7

只有改革创新，才能有效挖掘、组合和利用自然资源和人力资源。

Only through reform and innovation can we explore, combine and utilize *natural and human resources*.

◇ 例 8

在实现共同富裕过程中，人民美好生活需要日益广泛，既对物质生活也对精神生活提出更高要求。因此，共同富裕不仅是指人民在物质层面上的富裕，也是指人民在精神层面上的富足。

In the process of achieving common prosperity, the people have an increasingly extensive need for a better life, and a higher demand on both *material and cultural life*. Therefore, common prosperity refers to both the people's *material and cultural affluence*.

◇ 例 9

要充分发挥国内市场和国际市场作用，利用好国内资源和国际资源，促进经济社会健康发展。

We should give full play to the role of *the domestic and international market* and make full use of *domestic and international resources* to promote the healthy development of economy and society.

◇ 例 10

中国电信拥有全球规模最大的宽带互联网络和技术领先的移动通信网络，具备为全球客户提供跨地域、全业务的综合信息服务能力和客户服务渠道体系，目前已成为全球最大的 LTE-FDD 4G 运营商、光纤宽带运营商、IPTV 运营商、固定电话运营商。

With the world's largest broadband Internet network and a leading-edge mobile communications network, China Telecom is capable of providing cross-region, fully integrated information services and a sound customer service channel system for global customers. Today, the company has become the world's largest *operator of LTE-FDD 4G*, *optical broadband*, *IPTV and fixed-line telephone*.

以上四个例子中，原文下划线的部分均由并列名词短语组成，其中有些名词核心词重复出现，有的还重复了多次（如例 10 的"运营商"）。这些名词如果都翻译出来，不符合英语的表达习惯，前文讲过，英文可以用多个定语修饰一个名词，而非重复这一名词。因此，中译英时，中文中重复的名词仅翻译一次，其他部分则省译，即"自然资源和人力资源"译为 natural and human resources，"国内市场和国际市场"译为 domestic and international market，"国内资源和国际资源"译为 domestic and international resources，"LTE-FDD 4G 运营商、光纤宽带运营商、IPTV 运营商、固定电话运营商"译为 operator of LTE-FDD 4G, optical broadband, IPTV and fixed-line telephone。这样译文更符合英文表达习惯，否则句子会显得冗余。

◆ 例 11
要提高我国参与全球治理的能力，着力增强<u>规则制定能力、议程设置能力、舆论宣传能力、统筹协调能力</u>。

We must improve our ability to participate in global governance, and in particular, *our ability to make rules, set agendas, and carry out publicity and coordination.*

例 11 原文中下划线部分，"能力"一词重复了多次，"能力"前面都是动词短语作定语，翻译时仅需翻译一次"能力"，后面用不定式作定语即可。

除不同定语加同一名词这一结构外，中文有时还会将两个或多个动宾短语并列，翻译时也要注意省译重复的名词。请看下面的例子。

◆ 例 12
人类可以<u>利用自然、改造自然</u>，但归根结底是自然的一部分，必须<u>呵护自然，不能凌驾于自然之上</u>。

Human beings can *use and transform nature*, but they are ultimately part of it, so they must *protect rather than override it.*

◇ 例 13

要公平分配好生态产品和享有生态产品，公平地获得绿水青山所带来的金山银山，进而实现全体老百姓的共同富裕。

We should *allocate and enjoy ecological products* equitably, and get equitably the "gold" and "silver" brought by clear waters and green mountains, so that all people will enjoy common prosperity.

以上两个例子中原文下划线部分均为动宾短语并列，宾语均为重复的同一名词，翻译时均做了一定的省译处理，即"利用自然、改造自然"译成了 use and transform nature，"呵护自然，不能凌驾于自然之上"译成了 protect rather than override it（由于前面刚刚提到 nature，所以这里用了代词 it），"分配好生态产品和享有生态产品"译成了 allocate and enjoy ecological products。这样的译文更符合英文特点，更为地道。

本章所涉及的中英文这一区别比较细微，需要翻译学习者平时注重观察，将本章所述技巧运用到翻译实践当中，从而提高自己的译文质量。

拓展练习

翻译下列句子，注意英语名词在译文中的重复和中文重复的名词在英语中的省译。

1. Various museums, galleries and other exhibition institutions open their doors and invite you to discover fascinating collections, and *permanent and special exhibitions*.
2. The restaurant WEINWIRTSCHAFT lounge & restaurant with show kitchen and sun terrace will spoil you with *international as well as regional dishes*.
3. Jungfrau Railways invested 470 Million Swiss Francs for better comfort and an improved *travel and shopping experience* for our visitors.
4. Often it is the enlarged scale or intensity of *application* of well-known technologies that result in world-wide effects.
5. Undoubtedly this tendency for joint action, too, will accelerate in the future as it

is realized that cooperative undertakings are essential if the benefits as well as the dangers of *global technologies* are to be met.

6. 但这种能力提出了相当重要的<u>技术问题和国际问题</u>。
7. 中美两国建交以来，双边经贸关系持续发展，<u>合作领域不断拓宽，合作水平不断提高</u>，形成了高度互补、利益交融的互利共赢关系，不仅两国受益，而且惠及全球。
8. 绿水青山既是<u>自然财富</u>、<u>生态财富</u>，又是社会财富、<u>经济财富</u>。
9. 但是，中华民族绝不会自甘沉沦，亡国灭种的危险深深刺痛了中华民族的神经，唤醒了隐藏深处的<u>民族意识和民族精神</u>。
10. 在农业文明阶段，人类开始利用自然，<u>逐步学会欣赏自然</u>。

参考译文与简析

1. 各种各样的博物馆、美术馆和其他展览机构敞开大门，邀请您探索迷人的收藏品，<u>参观永久展览和特别展览</u>。（原文中的 permanent and special exhibitions 译为"永久展览和特别展览"，重复"展览"一词更符合中文表达习惯。）
2. 葡萄酒世界（WEINWIRTSCHAFT）休闲餐厅建有展示厨房和阳光露台，供应的<u>异域菜肴和当地菜肴</u>，将使您大饱口福。（原文中的 international as well as regional dishes 译为"国际菜肴和地区菜肴"，"菜肴"一词重复。）
3. 少女峰铁路投资 4.7 亿瑞士法郎，为游客提供更舒适、更出色的<u>旅行体验和购物体验</u>。（travel and shopping experience 译为"旅行体验和购物体验"，重复"体验"一词。）
4. 通常，众所周知的技术更大范围的<u>应用</u>或更频繁的<u>使用</u>会产生遍及全球的影响。（根据中文的表达习惯，原文的 application 在译文中重复翻译，即"在更大范围的应用或更频繁的使用"。）
5. 毫无疑问，这种联合行动的趋势未来也会加速，因为人们认识到，如果要获得<u>全球技术</u>带来的利益，应对<u>全球技术</u>引发的危险，合作至关重要。（原文中的名词短语 global technologies 在译文中重复，使得表达更清晰。）
6. But such an ability raises rather important *technical and international issues*. （technical and international issues 译为"技术问题和国际问题"，"问题"一词重复。）

7. Since the establishment of diplomatic relations between China and the US, bilateral trade and economic relations have come a long way, with *expanding fields of cooperation at higher levels*. A mutually beneficial and win-win relationship with strong complementarity and interlinked interests has been forged, benefiting not only the two countries but also the entire world. （原文中的"合作"为重复表达，英译文中只使用了一次。）

8. Clear waters and green mountains are not only *natural and ecological wealth*, but also *social and economic wealth*. （原文中"财富"出现了四次，英译文中wealth仅使用了两次，这种省译符合英语的表达习惯。）

9. However, the Chinese nation never abandoned itself. The danger of national subjugation and genocide deeply stimulated the nerves of the Chinese and awakened the *national consciousness and spirit*. （"民族意识和民族精神"在译文中是national consciousness and spirit，原文重复使用"民族"一词，译文中仅用了一次。）

10. During the agricultural civilization period, human beings began to *use and learn to appreciate nature*. （原文中"自然"出现了两次，英译文中只出现了一次，符合英语表达习惯。）

第十三章　中文连动式的翻译

一、何为连动式？

所谓"连动式"就是指中文两个或两个以上的动词或动词短语并列使用，这些动词之间有时没有逗号，有时使用逗号。这些动词或动词短语连用，有时是真正的并列关系，有时却暗含时间顺序、目的、方式/手段、因果、伴随等关系，只不过中文形式上很少使用表示衔接关系的关联词。

◆ 例 1

他吃过早饭骑上自行车上学去了。（表时间先后和方式/手段）
After breakfast, he went to school by bike.

◆ 例 2

老栓接了，抖抖的装入衣袋，又在外面按了两下；便点上灯笼，吹熄灯盏，走向里屋子去了。（表时间先后）
After taking it, Laoshuan put the packet of coins in his pocket and patted the pocket twice. He then lit the paper lantern, blew out the lamp, and walked into the inner room.

◆ 例 3

中国一直致力于维护亚太地区的和平与稳定，坚持走和平发展道路，坚持互利共赢的开放战略，坚持在和平共处五项原则基础上同所有国家发展友好合作。（表并列）
China is committed to promoting peace and stability in the Asian-Pacific Region, pursuing the path of peaceful development, the mutually beneficial strategy

of opening up, and cooperation with all countries on the basis of the Five Principles of Peaceful Coexistence.

◇ 例 4

他找了一些干苔藓、枯枝等取火烧水。（表目的）

He collected some dry moss and branches to make fire and boil water.

◇ 例 5

老张连续几天熬夜加班工作，累病了，今天没法来上班。（表因果）

Having worked all night for days, Mr. Zhang is ill, so he cannot come today.

从上面的例子可以看出，中文的连动式可以表示各种关系，这是因为中文不注重形式上的衔接，而注重意思连贯；不注重主从结构的呈现，更倾向使用并列结构。所以，这些连动式之间到底是何种关系要靠读者去体会和分析。然而，如果将连动式翻译成英语，就要考虑中英文之间表达形式的差别，大多数连动式不能直接译成英语的并列结构。

二、如何翻译连动式？

翻译中文的连动式，首先要弄清楚这些看似并列的动词或动词短语之间是何种关系，因为和前文所述中文特点不同，英文表达意思上的连贯取决于形式上的衔接，和中文相比，英文更注重主从结构。因此，只有分析出连动式之间的逻辑关系，才能准确将其译成英文。主要方法如下。

1. 译成英文并列短语

如果中文中的连动式表示并列关系或者动作发生的先后顺序，而且都表示动作或状态，则可以译为英语的并列结构。请看下面的例子。

◇ 例 6

我们过了江，进了车站。

We crossed the river and entered the station.

◇ 例 7

长沙蛮反，寇益阳。（长沙蛮人反叛，进攻益阳。）

The minority tribes of Changsha revolted and attacked Yiyang.

◇ 例 8

二十世纪 60 年代，贝德高教授在莫斯科大学东方语言学院学习汉语，毕业之后在符拉迪沃斯托克远东大学中文系任教并出任系主任。

Professor Pildegovics studied the Chinese language at Eastern Languages Institute of Moscow University in the 1960s, and after graduation, became a teacher and director of Chinese Language Department at Vladivostok Far East University.

以上三个例子中下划线部分的动词基本表示动作的先后顺序或者并列关系，而且基本都表示动作，因此译为英语的并列结构。

2. 译成英文的主从结构

中文大多数连动式不能译为英文的并列结构，而应译为英文的主从结构，主要有以下几种情况。

（1）有些连动式虽然表示先后关系，但如果有的动词表示动作，有的动词表示状态，其中表示状态的动词可以译为从属部分（例如分词）等。请看下面的例子。

◇ 例 9

山桃儿望着街上来来往往的车，感觉到自己的双腿有点困，就坐在药铺前的台阶上休息。

Looking at the cars running on the street, Shantao felt tired, so she sat down on a step in front of the herbal medicine shop to have a rest.

这个例子中，下划线部分的动词虽然表示先后顺序，但也蕴含着主从关系，而且前面两个动词表示状态，后面的"坐"实际上是表示"坐下"的动作，最后"休息"表示目的，因此没有译成并列结构。

◇ 例 10

我打了一个呵欠,点起一支烟,喷出烟来,对着灯默默地敬奠这些苍翠精致的英雄们。

I yawned, lit a cigarette and puffed out some smoke, giving a silent salute to these green delicate heroes.

这个例子原文前三个动词表示动作,最后一个动词表示状态,因此将前三个动词译成并列谓语,最后一个动词译成现在分词短语,表示伴随。

(2)有些连动式之间实际上暗含原因、时间、方式、目的等关系,这样的连动式也需要根据情况译成主从结构。

◇ 例 11

中国秉持绿色、共享、开放、廉洁的办奥理念,全力克服新冠肺炎疫情影响,认真兑现对国际社会的庄严承诺,确保了北京冬奥会如期顺利举行。

Committed to organizing a green, inclusive, open and clean Games, China has made every effort to counter the impact of COVID-19, fulfilled its solemn pledge to the international community, and ensured the smooth opening of the Beijing Olympic Winter Games as scheduled.

例 11 中,原文"秉持……理念"是后面下划线动词的方式,因此将这一部分译为分词短语作为从属部分,其他动词译成并列结构。

◇ 例 12

近一年来,中国持续强化关键信息基础设施保护,开展覆盖全国的关键信息基础设施网络安全检查,深入排查重点领域、重要行业关键信息基础设施的网络安全风险隐患,提高网络安全防护能力。

Over the past year, China has reinforced the protection of critical information infrastructure, carried out nationwide cyber security examinations of the infrastructure, and checked the risks of cyber security concerning such infrastructure of key areas and industries to enhance the capability of cyber security protection.

例 12 中，最后一个动词短语是原文前三个下划线动词的目的，即"提高网络安全防护能力"，因此，翻译时将前三个动词译成并列谓语，最后的动词译成不定式作目的状语。

✧ 例 13

明白了这种关系，不但可以解决疑问，增长知识，并且同时还可以利用新得的知识，去弥补感官的缺陷，扩张人类的势力，征服自然的环境。

When we understand the relationship, we can not only solve our problems and enrich our knowledge but also make use of the new knowledge to make up the shortcomings of our senses, expand our influence and conquer nature.

该例中，"明白了这种关系"和后面的动词短语之间在逻辑上并不是并列关系，而是指时间先后顺序，所以翻译为时间状语，后半部分"去弥补感官的缺陷，扩张人类的势力，征服自然的环境"又是"利用新得的知识"这一动词短语的目的，因此后半部分译为英语不定式作目的状语。

✧ 例 14

强盗听到这个消息，感到惭愧和后悔，就到姜肱的学舍来拜见他，叩头谢罪，奉还所抢走的衣物。

Hearing the news, the robbers felt ashamed and regretful, so they came to Jiang Gong's schoolhouse, bowed to apologize and returned the clothes they had taken.

该句原文连动式较多，共有六个。其中"感到……"属于状态动词，"听到……消息"属于动作动词，翻译时处理为主从结构。后面"到……拜见"是前面动作的结果，用 so 作连词（当然，英语中 so 是并列连词）。"谢罪"是"叩头"的目的，因此用不定式。

（3）如果连动式是以下几种情况，一般也要译成英文的主从结构："是"动词和其他动词构成连动式；过去的动作和现在的动作构成连动式；主动和被动构成连动式。请分别看下面的例子。

✧ 例 15

达坂城风力发电站<u>位于</u>乌鲁木齐市区与达坂城区之间的公路旁，<u>由</u>数百座巨大的发电风车<u>组成</u>，<u>是</u>全国最大的风能基地。

Situated by the expressway connecting downtown Urumqi and Dabancheng District, Dabancheng Wind Farm, consisting of hundreds of gigantic wind turbines, is China's largest wind-power base.

这个例子中，原文前面两个划线的动词是动作词，最后一个是"是"动词，而且"位于"一般会用被动形式，因此可将三个连动式处理为主从结构，并保证句式的平衡。

✧ 例 16

该沙漠<u>形成</u>于汉代，<u>是</u>浓缩了世界各大沙漠典型景观的博物馆，更<u>是</u>诠释古楼兰王国消失的最后一片圣地。

The desert, formed during the Han Dynasty, is a museum containing sights typical of major world deserts around the world, and the last sacred ground of the ancient Loulan Kingdom.

这个例子的原文包含三个连动式，第一个是动作词，而且是过去的动作，后两个为"是"动词，因此将过去的动作译为从属结构（使用过去分词），后面两个"是"动词跟的都是名词，最好译为并列结构。

✧ 例 17

长城<u>形成于</u>公元前五世纪，现在每天<u>吸引</u>着成千上万的游客。

The Great Wall, which came into being in the fifth century B.C., attracts tens of thousands of visitors every day.

这个例子的原文中，第一个动词是过去的动作，第二个动词表示现在，因此不能译成并列结构，而应译成主从结构。一般表示过去的动作要变成从属结构，这里过去的动作"形成于"如果译成 come into being，不能使用分词，应考虑使用非限定性关系从句。

◆ 例 18

强盗<u>听</u>后很<u>受感动</u>，便将他俩都<u>释放</u>了，只将衣服和财物<u>抢光</u>。

Moved by what they had said, the robbers released both of them, only taking away their clothes and possessions.

该句原文有四个连动式，"受感动"为被动结构，后面的"释放"和"抢光"是主动结构，所以三个动词不能译成并列结构。另外，动词"听"可以和"受感动"连在一起，不必译出。

3. 拆分成不同的英文句子

当中文连动式暗含的关系不是并列关系，或者前后意思并不十分连贯，或者连动式较多时，就需要考虑拆句。请看下面的例子：

◆ 例 19

王冕自此在秦家<u>放牛</u>，每日黄昏<u>回家</u>，跟着母亲<u>歇宿</u>。

Wang Mian became a herdsman of the Qin family. He would go home every evening and sleep at home.

这个例子的第一部分和后面的两部分显然不在同一层面，因此翻译时需要拆句。

◆ 例 20

漠河，<u>位于</u>中国最北端，<u>隶属于</u>黑龙江大兴安岭地区，与内蒙古<u>相邻</u>，与俄罗斯<u>隔江相望</u>，在这可以<u>看到</u>"极昼"和"北极光"两大奇景。

Mohe City belongs to Daxing'anling Prefecture of Heilongjiang Province.

It adjoins Inner Mongolia, separated from Russia by a river. It is home to the wonderous midnight sun and polar lights.

这一部分的前两个连动式（位于……，隶属于……）可以看作是一个层次，中间两个连动式（与……相邻，与……相望）为一个层次，最后一个连动式（看到……）为一个层次，因此译成了三个英文句子。

✧ 例 21

面对人类未知的新冠病毒，中国坚持以科学为先导，充分运用近年来科技创新成果，组织协调全国优势科研力量，以武汉市为主战场，统筹全国和疫情重灾区，根据疫情发展不同阶段确定科研攻关重点，坚持科研、临床、防控一线相互协同和产学研各方紧密配合，为疫情防控提供了有力科技支撑。

Confronted by Covid-19, a previously unknown virus, China has exploited the pioneering role of science and technology and fully applied the results of scientific and technical innovation in recent years. Top scientific research resources have been gathered from around the nation to support virus control. Focusing on the main battlefield of Wuhan and coordinating efforts in the most severely-affected areas and across the rest of the country, China pinpointed key R&D areas for different stages of virus control. The close coordination between scientific research, clinical application, and frontline virus control, and between enterprises, universities, and research institutes, has given powerful support for the war against the virus.

该句原文属于中文报告中典型的句式，连动式较多，使得句子较长，翻译时需要做适当拆句处理。

总之，连动式是中文表达中非常明显的特点之一，这和中文注重动态和并列的特点有关，但译为英文时不能将这些连动式也像流水一般罗列，而是需要根据情况进行变通。

拓展练习

翻译下列句子，请注意中文连动式的处理。

1. 面对疫情，中国人民万众一心、众志成城，取得了抗击疫情重大战略成果。
2. 桦林雪雕娱乐园位于市区西北部的桦林公园内，是新疆最大的雪雕游乐园。
3. 雾凇岛原名卧龙岛，位于吉林市西北 35 千米的乌拉街满族自治镇（乌拉古城）境内，是松花江上一个江心小岛。
4. 中国本着依法、公开、透明、负责任态度，第一时间向国际社会通报疫情信息，毫无保留同各方分享防控和救治经验。
5. 中国把人民生命安全和身体健康放在第一位，以坚定果敢的勇气和决心，采取最全面最严格最彻底的防控措施，有效阻断病毒传播链条。
6. 亚布力滑雪场位于尚志市东南部亚布力镇大锅盔山北麓，属张广才岭支脉，西距哈尔滨市 200 千米，东离牡丹江市 120 千米，是目前中国最大的综合性滑雪训练和比赛基地及南极训练基地。
7. 脱贫攻坚战对中国农村的改变是历史性的、全方位的，是中国农村的又一次伟大革命，深刻改变了贫困地区落后面貌，有力推动了中国农村整体发展，补齐了全面建成小康社会最突出短板，为全面建设社会主义现代化国家、实现第二个百年奋斗目标奠定了坚实基础。
8. 他们将积极开展人文交流项目，扩大来华夏令营、"孔子学院奖学金"规模；将大力支持开发"一带一路"沿线国家双语教材以及文化服务项目和中外文对照辞典等。
9. 我们应该树立命运与共的理念，改变独善其身的意识，摒弃二元对立的思维，推动构建人类命运共同体、携手建设美好世界。
10. 不同国家的政党应增进互信、加强沟通、密切协作，探索在新型国际关系的基础上建立求同存异、相互尊重、互学互鉴的新型政党关系，汇聚构建人类命运共同体的强大力量。

参考译文与简析

1. Confronted by this virus, the Chinese people, having joined together as one and united their efforts, have succeeded in containing the spread of the virus.（该句有

三个小分句，"面对疫情"显然是状语，主结构应该是"中国人民取得了……成果"，"万众一心、众志成城"译为伴随状语。）

2. Birch Forest Snow Sculpture Park, located in Birch Forest Park in the northwest of the city proper, is the largest snow-sculpture park in Xinjiang.（该句存在两个动词"位于"和"是"，分析后可以确定一个主结构，另一个变成从属结构。该译文将后半部分作为主结构，"位于……"变成过去分词作后置定语。）

3. Rime Island, previously known as Wolong Island, is located in Wulajie Manchu Autonomous Town（also known as Wula Old Town）, which is 35 km away from the northwest of Jilin City. It is an island in the middle of the Songhua River.（前半部分的主谓结构为"雾凇岛位于乌拉街满族自治镇"，后半部分单独成句。）

4. In an open, transparent, and responsible manner, China, in accordance with the law, gave timely notification to the international community of the onset of a new coronavirus, and shared without reserve its experience in containing the spread of the virus and treating the infected.（该句中"本着……态度"显然要翻译成状语，后面两个连动式译成并列结构。）

5. Making people's lives and health its first priority, China, by adopting extensive, stringent, and thorough containment measures, has succeeded in cutting all channels for the transmission of the virus.（该句的连动式中"把……放在第一位"译成状语，后面"有效阻断病毒传播链条"应该是主结构，中间的动词译为方式状语。）

6. Yabuli Ski Resort is located in Yabuli Town in southeast Shangzhi City, at the northern foot of the Daguokui Mountain of the Zhangguangcai Range. 200 km to the east of Harbin and 120 km to the west of Mudanjiang, it is China's largest skiing training and competition base and Antarctic training base.（本句翻译时作了拆句处理，拆分之后的两部分分别使用一个主结构，其他动词短语变成从属结构，有些动词省译。）

7. The battle against poverty has been another great revolution in rural China, leading to historic and comprehensive changes. The campaign put an end to the backwardness of poverty-stricken areas, boosted overall rural development, resolved the greatest threat to success in achieving moderate prosperity in all respects, and

laid a solid foundation for building a modern socialist China and realizing the Second Centenary Goal. （该句原文较长，由多个动词短语组成连动式。翻译时需要先分析句子之间的逻辑关系，否则会无从下手。经过分析，会发现从开头到"一次伟大革命"可以看作总说，后面几个并列结构是具体体现。这样，原句就译成了两个英语句子。）

8. They will conduct people-to-people and cultural exchange programs and expand the scale of summer camps in China and the Confucius Institute Scholarships. They will support cultural services and bilingual textbooks and dictionaries compilation in both Chinese and foreign languages for countries along the "Belt and Road". （该句中的分号在英语中可以转译为句号，这样原文一句话就译成了英语两句话。第一句话中依然包含连动式，译成并列结构即可。）

9. We should foster and embrace the idea of interconnectivity of interests and a shared future in place of the self-concern mindset and dichotomic mentality, and promote the building of a community with a shared future for humankind and a better world. （原句中有些动词意思相近，翻译时需要简化，如"树立……理念""改变……意识"和"摒弃……思维"，以及"推动构建"和"携手建设"，简化后根据原文的意思将连动式译成并列动词结构。）

10. Political parties from different countries should enhance mutual trust, strengthen communication, and work closely to forge, on the basis of a new form of international relations, a new form of party-to-party relations featuring the seeking of common grounds beyond differences, mutual respect and mutual learning, so as to create a mighty force that enables us to build a community with shared future for humankind. （分析原文后会发现，最后一个动词短语"汇聚……强大力量"可以看作是前面动词的目的，放在最后用不定式形式作目的状语，前面基本使用并列结构。）

第十四章　中文范畴名词省译和英译中添加范畴名词

范畴名词指用来表示行为、现象、属性等的词，是中文常用的特指手段。范畴名词一般放在动词或形容词的后面，有些也放在名词后面。有时前面有助词"的"，有时没有。其中最常用的有"行为""态度""方面""方式""局面""情景""情况""现象""工作""方面""态度"等。一般情况下，这些范畴名词在句中没有实际意义，只是使中文句子更加流畅。翻译时，中文句子中这类范畴名词一般应省译，否则英文会显得冗余。相反，有些英文句子翻译为中文时添加一定的范畴名词会让中译文更通顺。

一、中文范畴名词省译

中文的范畴名词大多只是用来使句子更通顺、更流畅，并没有实际意义。这些词译成英文时，一般需要省译，如果译出会显得冗余。如"百家争鸣的局面"可以直接译为 contention of a hundred schools of thought，"局面"省译；再比如，"管理工作"直接译为 management，而不是 management work，"童年的情景"可以直接译为 childhood，而非 the scene of childhood，等等。请看下面更多的例句。

◇ 例1

酒店营销不仅仅是单一的推销模式，它涉及的面广而深，包含市场营销的调查，饭店产品的设计、开发和定价，产品推销，产品流通等方面的内容。

Hotel marketing is more than just a single marketing model, but it covers a wide and deep range of areas, including marketing research, hotel product design, development and pricing, and product marketing and circulation.

这个例子中，原文的"等方面的内容"是为了把前面列举的"市场营销的调查，饭店产品的设计、开发和定价，产品推销，产品流通"做一个收尾，加上这几个字会使中文行文更完整，但并没有实际意义，翻译时做省译处理。

◇ 例2

经过艰苦卓绝的努力，中国付出巨大代价和牺牲，有力扭转了疫情局势，用一个多月的时间初步遏制了疫情蔓延<u>势头</u>。

Through painstaking efforts and a heavy price, China has succeeded in turning the situation around. In little more than a single month, the spread of the virus was contained.

该例原文在"疫情蔓延"后面添加了"势头"二字，也是为了使表达更完整，实际上没有任何实际意义，因此，译文中也做了省译处理。

◇ 例3

失业<u>问题</u>比通胀<u>问题</u>更为严重，因为失业<u>问题</u>涉及社会治安<u>问题</u>。

Unemployment is a more serious problem than inflation, for the former is related to public security.

该例原文中有四个"问题"，实际上只译出了一个，其他省译即可。

◇ 例4

落实依法治国基本方略，加快建设社会主义法治国家，必须全面推进科学立法、严格执法、公正司法、全民守法<u>进程</u>。

To implement the rule of law as the basic strategy, and accelerate the building of a law-based socialist country, we should make laws through proper procedures, enforce them strictly, administer justice impartially, and ensure that everyone abides by the law.

"进程"也是中文常见的范畴名词，它前面通常是一个动词，两个词合在一起构成名词短语，实际上"进程"本身没有实际意义，翻译时应省译。

◆ 例 5

在公费医疗制度下，"一人看病全家吃药"的现象很多。

In the old public-funded medical care system, it was common that a person who was entitled to free medical care would have medicine prescribed in his or her name for all his or her family members.

"现象"也是中文很常见的一个范畴名词，大多数情况下没有实际意义。如"铺张浪费现象""乱砍滥伐现象""失业现象"等，翻译时需要省译，不必译成 phenomenon。

二、英译中时添加范畴名词

由前面的分析可以看出，范畴名词在中文中很常见，翻译时对该类词要进行省译处理。英译中时，有些由动词或形容词添加后缀变来的名词在句子中作主语、宾语或表语，如果翻译时仍然需要这类名词作主语、宾语或表语，不妨在中译文后面添加范畴名词，以符合中文的表达习惯，如：oxidation（氧化作用）、resistance（阻力问题/现象）、defence（防御工事）、unemployment（失业问题/现象）。

◆ 例 6

The soaps are reformed and given to families with children in need to improve *hygiene* locally and fight against the spread of disease.

这些肥皂经过改造，分发给有孩子的家庭，以改善当地的卫生状况，预防疾病传播。

这里的 improve hygiene，译成"改善卫生"就不如译成"改善卫生状况"或者"改善卫生条件"更符合中文的表达习惯，所以范畴名词"状况"或"条件"在译文中显得必不可少。

◇ 例 7

Between the three inner worlds, the earth, Mars, and Venus, communication delay will never be more than twenty minutes—not enough to interfere seriously with *commerce or administration*, but more than sufficient to shatter those personal links of sound or vision that can give us a sense of direct contact with friends on earth, wherever they may be.

太阳系内层的地球、火星和金星之间，通讯延迟永远不会超过 20 分钟——不足以严重阻碍商业或管理活动，却足以打断个人之间的声音或视觉联系，但正是这种联系使我们和地球上的朋友有一种直接接触的感觉，无论朋友身处地球上的哪一个角落。

这里的 commerce or administration 译成"商业或管理活动"显然比"商业和管理"要通顺得多。"活动"一词就是范畴名词。

◇ 例 8

Its mission is to create an eco-sensitive international village, which focuses on the training of women and youth in ecological issues and sustainable development, in conflict prevention and peace, as well as in conflict resolution.

其任务就是建立具有强烈生态意识的国际村，为妇女和青年提供有关生态问题和可持续发展、防止冲突与争取和平以及解决冲突等方面的培训。

◇ 例 9

The program focused on agriculture, information technology, environment protection, and sustainable development.

该计划重点放在农业、信息技术、环境保护和可持续发展等方面。

例 8 和例 9 原文中的 in ecological issues and sustainable development, in conflict prevention and peace, as well as in conflict resolution 和 agriculture, information technology, environment protection, and sustainable development 列举了培训和计划的不同方面，因此，译文在最后添加"方面"一词作为总结，显得更为通顺。

✧ 例 10

Any attempts at really improving the total catch will depend not only on improved technology; they will depend directly on more ecological knowledge, more efficient fishery methods, controlled competition, and conservation.

任何真正提高总捕捞量的尝试不仅取决于技术改进，还将直接取决于更丰富的生态知识、更有效的捕捞方法、受限的竞争和保护情况。

这里，如果将最后的 conservation 直接译为"保护"，句子读起来显然会显得不完整，加上范畴名词"情况"，译文会变得地道得多。

✧ 例 11

Technology will raise more problems of overpopulation and environmental pollution.

技术会引起更多人口过剩和环境污染问题。

该例译文中最后添加了范畴名词"问题"，整句译文读起来显然比"技术会引起更多人口过剩和环境污染"要通顺得多。

本章主要探讨了中文范畴名词的省译和英语一些抽象名词在中译文中的范畴化。了解英汉这一差异对于避免翻译中出现 Chinglish（中式英语）和欧化的中文句子非常有帮助。

拓展练习

翻译下列句子，请注意范畴名词的省译和添加。

1. From 1977 to 1997, he taught and conducted research on computer-controlled artificial environments.
2. Hisense Imp. & Exp. Co., Ltd. was established in 1991 and is responsible for the export of televisions, air conditioners, refrigerators, computers, and cordless telephones.

3. I have had room only to deal with a few broad topics—environment alteration, ocean resources, outer space. One could also add natural resource management, population growth, information-processing, genetic engineering, and, of course, military technology as areas in which the need for some international regulatory machinery is equally clear.

4. His vast corpus of work (including over thirty books) also addressed drama, cultural theory, the environment, the English novel, the development of language, leftist politics and, in the period before his death, Welshness.

5. She could feel swift anger stir, even at this late date, as she thought of that night but she subdued it and tossed her head until the earrings danced.

6. 在中美经贸关系发展历程中,也曾多次出现波折、面临困难局面。两国本着理性、合作的态度,通过对话协商解决问题,化解了矛盾、缩小了分歧,双边经贸关系更趋成熟。

7. 在生态环境保护问题上,发展中国家存在的问题较为严重。

8. 由于认错态度诚恳,李长史放了李白一马,没有处罚他。

9. 近年来,国内投资和消费需求均呈较快增长态势。

10. 发展问题一直是世界各国普遍关注的问题。大部分发展中国家取得独立后,在发展民族经济、改变贫穷落后面貌、缩小同发达国家的经济差距等方面,取得了巨大成绩。

参考译文与简析

1. 1977年至1997年间,他在计算机控制的人工环境领域从事教学和研究工作。(taught and conducted research 译为"从事教学和研究工作"其中"工作"就是添加的范畴名词。)

2. 海信进出口公司成立于1991年,负责电视机、空调、冰箱、电脑以及无线电话机等产品的出口业务。(英文句中列举了很多细分产品,译成中文时,为了使中文表达连贯就添加了"等产品",其中"产品"就是范畴名词。另外,export 译成了"出口业务",添加了范畴名词"业务"。)

3. 由于篇幅有限,这里只能讨论几个宽泛的主题,包括环境改变、海洋资源和外太空问题,实际上还可以加上自然资源管理、人口增长、信息处理、遗传工程等问题，当然还有军事技术问题，这些领域同样需要一些国际监管机制。（译文中有三处都添加了范畴名词"问题"，使得中译文读起来清楚、连贯。）

4. 他著述颇丰，共出版30余部著作，还涉及戏剧、文化理论、环境、英语小说、语言发展、左翼政治等主题，去世前那段时间，他还研究了威尔士问题。（该句翻译时添加了范畴名词"主题"和"问题"，使行文更通顺。如果不添加这两个范畴名词，中译文会显得生硬拗口。）

5. 她感到怒火中烧，即使迟至今日，一想到那天晚上的情形，她就感到非常生气，但还是压住了怒火，把头一扬，耳环也跟着跳动起来。（thought of that night 译为"一想到那天晚上的情形"，更符合中文的表达习惯。其中添加的"情形"就是范畴名词。）

6. The history of China-US trade and economic relations has seen twists and turns and difficult situations. Through rationality and cooperation, the two countries have managed to resolve previous conflicts, bridge differences, and render the bilateral commercial relationship more mature through dialogue and consultation. （中文句子中的"局面""态度"都是范畴名词，翻译时省译。）

7. As for ecosystem protection, there are serious problems in developing countries. （"在生态环境保护问题上"中的"问题"属于范畴名词，翻译时省译。）

8. Thanks to his sincere apology, he was forgiven by the local official Mr. Li. （原句中的"态度"是范畴名词，翻译时省译。）

9. In recent years, both the domestic investment and consumption have been growing rapidly. （原句中的"态势"是范畴名词，翻译时省译。）

10. Development is always a universal concern. Since they became independent, most of developing countries have made progress in developing their economy, reducing their poverty and narrowing the gap between themselves and developed countries. （原句中"发展问题"中的"问题"和"改变贫穷落后面貌"中的"面貌"属于范畴名词，翻译时省译。）

第十五章　英译中修辞增译和中译英修辞省译

英汉两种语言相比，英文更注重信息和写实，中文更注重艺术和渲染。因此，英文译为中文时，在意思不变的前提下，有时要添加一些渲染的词汇，以迎合中文读者的思维方式和审美预期，特别是散文和宣传类文本；相反，中文译成英文时，在意思不变的前提下，往往要省译一些描述和渲染类词汇，特别是诗歌、散文、宣传类文本。这种情况可以分别叫作"修辞增译"和"修辞省译"。比如，英文中 have fun exploring Switzerland 译成"探索瑞士玩得愉快"就不如"享受探索瑞士带来的无限乐趣"，history of this ancient art 译成"古老艺术的历史"就不如"古老艺术的悠久历史"更地道。相反，中文"寒天或阴雨绵绵的日子"译成英文只能是 cold or rainy days，其中"绵绵"在英语中没有对应词；如果旅游文本中出现了"身临其间，思古抚今，会令人感慨万千"，则整个部分都可以省译。

一、英译中修辞增译

根据原文文本类型所表达出的语气以及中文注重艺术和审美的特点，英译中有时要增译一定的动词、形容词、副词等，以符合中文相对应的文本类型的语气以及中文读者的审美预期。请看下面的例子。

◇ 例 1

In the evening, after the banquets, the concerts and the table tennis exhibitions, he would work on the drafting of the final communiqué.

晚上，<u>参加</u>宴会、<u>出席</u>音乐会、<u>观看</u>乒乓球表演后，他还得起草最后公报。

◇ 例2

We expect Chinese guests to put a higher value on cleanliness and safety, authentic and exclusive experiences, smaller groups, nature activities and last but not least: sustainability.

我们预计中国游客将更重视清洁和安全，更在意真实和独特的体验，更愿意参加小团队旅行，更喜欢自然活动，更注重可持续性。

◇ 例3

The wine route of East Switzerland leads from Schaffhausen to St. Gallen, through vineyards, past scenic sights and *picturesque* villages. Cosy inns and restaurants invite you to take a break along the way, *including a feast for your taste buds.*

瑞士东部的葡萄酒线路从沙夫豪森通往圣加仑，途经壮丽的葡萄园、风景优美的名胜以及如诗如画的村庄。舒适的旅馆和餐厅邀请您沿途小憩，并享受一场味蕾盛宴。

以上三个例子原文有的出自散文，有的出自旅游宣传文本，译文均根据文本类型以及中文读者的审美预期增加了下划线部分的动词。当然，例3还将 picturesque 译成了"如诗如画"，按照中文的表达习惯增译了"如诗"二字。

有时将英语译成中文时，如果里面含有复数名词，要适当添加表示数量的词，Years have passed 显然不能译成"年过去了"，而应译为"多年过去了"。再看下面一个例子，其中的"万"和"千"就属于增译。

◇ 例4

The very earth trembled as with the tramps of horses and murmur of angry men.

连大地都震动了，仿佛万马奔腾，千夫怒吼。

当然，英译中最常见的修辞增译便是增加形容词和副词，特别是宣传类文本的翻译。请看下面的例子。

◇ 例 5

Nestled among golden forests, mountains and glaciers, Saas-Fee serves as an ideal base camp for exploring the Saas Valley.

萨斯斐偎依在金色森林、巍峨高山和壮丽冰川组成的怀抱，堪称探索萨斯谷的理想出发地。

◇ 例 6

In between, the journey leads you through picturesque villages, diverse landscapes and cultural and culinary highlights.

在此期间，将穿越如诗如画的村庄和多姿多彩的美景，感受丰富多彩的文化亮点和美食亮点。

◇ 例 7

The trail leads you along idyllic river banks through autumnal vineyards up to Hohenklingen Castle.

小径带您沿田园诗般的河岸穿过秋季绚丽多彩的葡萄园，到达荷恩克林根城堡。

◇ 例 8

If you prefer two-wheeled transport, you will find a few inspirations for active voyages of discovery below. From a day at the bike park in Leysin to varied tours around Les Paccots or fast-paced Enduro trails in the Valais—there's something for everyone.

如果更喜欢将自行车作为交通工具，下面的信息可以为您提供探索之旅的灵感。从莱森自行车公园的一日游到莱斯帕科茨周边的各种旅行，再到瓦莱州快节奏的耐力自行车小径——这里提供适合每位游客的不同选择。

以上四个例子中，例 5 的译文"巍峨"和"壮丽"在英文中没有对应的单词，为了和前面的"金色"对应，所以添加这两个形容词，一方面使句子的节奏更平衡，一方面也使得译文更符合中文读者的审美预期。例 6 译文中的"如诗""多彩"和"丰富多彩"都是增译的形容词，使宣传的文字更具美感。当然，该例的译文中还添加了动词"感受"，和前文的"穿越"对应。例7译文中的"绚丽多彩"和例8中的"不同"也属于修辞增译。

◇ 例 9

Fine arts, photography and contemporary art brought together in one single spot near Lausanne station, in a cultural area that is unique in Switzerland.

美术、摄影和当代艺术在洛桑车站附近完美汇集在一起，形成瑞士独一无二的文化区。

◇ 例 10

It is one of the thriving leaders among Central European construction companies, characterized by sustainable growth of production performance and market value, with management levels meeting EU standards.

该公司是中欧建筑公司的龙头企业，业务蓬勃发展，市场业绩和市场价值持续增长，管理水平完全符合欧盟标准。

◇ 例 11

Visitors can experience the region's traditional architecture combined with modern art, as well as the beautiful natural surroundings of Parco Val Calanca.

游客可以体验该地区传统建筑与现代艺术的巧妙融合，尽情欣赏卡兰卡山谷公园优美的自然环境。

以上三个例子中的译文均增译了副词，分别是"完美""完全""巧妙"和"尽情"，旨在渲染语气，符合中文读者的表达习惯。当然，例11的译文还增加了动词"欣赏"，与前面的"体验"对应。

英译中时还会根据行文的需要添加叠词，叠词是中文的一大特色，也是使文字更加优美的一种手段，如"熠熠生辉"中的"熠熠"，"白雪皑皑"中的"皑皑"。英文中描写雪山经常会用 snowy mountains 或 snow-covered mountains，我们不妨将其译为"白雪皑皑的高山"。再看下面的例子，译文中"闪闪"就属于修辞增译。

◆ 例 12

Stroll through the gardens of the Arenenberg estate, past maple trees that seem almost gilded in the sunshine.

漫步在阿伦嫩堡庄园的花园中，经过阳光下金光闪闪的枫树。

通过前面的例子分析可以看出，英译中时很多修辞增译十分必要，这样才能保证译文符合中文的表达习惯和中文读者的审美预期，否则译文就像"白开水"，不太容易引起中文读者的共鸣，文学作品就无法带来审美的愉悦，宣传文本就无法在中文读者中起到宣传的作用。

二、中译英时的修辞省译

既然英译中的修辞增译不可避免，那么中译英时修辞省译也就不可避免了，因为英文本身不像中文那样注重审美。为使中文的英译文更好地为英文读者接受，更好地起到交流作用，很多时候必须采取修辞省译。中译英时的修辞省译不仅见于散文文本和宣传文本，其他文本的翻译也会有这种现象。

首先，中译英时要省译一些用于渲染语气的程度副词和形容词，如"大力""深刻""广泛""尽情"等。请看下面的例子。

◆ 例 13

发展问题是世界各国普遍关注的问题。
Development is a concern of all countries. / Development is a universal concern.

◆ 例 14

维护社会和谐稳定是香港保持良好营商环境、发展经济、改善民生的基本要求，符合广大香港同胞的根本利益。

Social stability and harmony is the basic requirement for business operation, economic development and the people's livelihood improvement in Hong Kong, according to the interests of the people there.

以上两个例子原文中的副词"普遍"和形容词"广大"均做了省译处理，这是因为原文中这两个词只是为了加强渲染的语气，没有实际意义。

其次，中译英时需要省译一些语义重复但旨在增强渲染和审美意味的词汇。请看下面的例子。

◇ 例 15

在转变外贸增长方式、扩大进口、加强知识产权保护，为全球贸易和世界经济继续作出贡献的同时，巨大的国内需求和广阔的国内市场是中国经济发展的持续动力，这就决定了中国的发展应当而且有可能实现以国内需求为主。

China is transforming its foreign trade growth mode, expanding its import, strengthening its intellectual property protection and thus continuously contributing to the world's trade and economy. Meanwhile, its huge domestic demand and market is the sustaining driving force for its economic growth, which determines that its development should and can rely on its domestic demand.

该例中，"全球"和"世界"意思重复，"巨大"和"广阔"意思重复，原文这样使用旨在增强渲染的语气，但英译文如果选取不同的形容词进行翻译就显得冗余，因此做了适当的省译处理。

◇ 例 16

为了避免"有增长、无发展"的现象，世界各国都把可持续发展作为国家宏观经济发展战略的一种重要选择，并深刻认识到，人类需要一个持续发展的途径。这是人类发展观的重大转折，具有深远的历史意义。

To avoid growth without development, all countries take sustainable development as one of their macro-economic development strategies and realize that human beings need an approach to such development. This marks a turning point in the outlook on human development, which is of historic significance.

该例原文中的"深刻"和"重大"旨在渲染语气,"深远的"和"历史"意思重复,这里的"历史"指的是"产生深远影响"的意思。鉴于此,译文做了适当省译处理。

✧ 例 17

苏州,是吴文化的<u>重要</u>发源地。苏绣、绘画、篆刻、昆曲、评弹、苏剧以及饮食、服饰、语言等融汇成其<u>丰富</u>内涵。

Suzhou is the cradle of Wu Culture, which covers the local embroidery, painting and seal cutting, Kunqu Opera, pingtan (ballad singing in local dialect), and Suzhou Opera, as well as local gastronomy, costume and dialect.

该例中的"重要"和"丰富"都是渲染语气的词语,没有实际意义,翻译时要做省译处理。

中文中还有一些四字格的成语前后两个字基本是一个意思。这样的"意复"四字成语在英语中一般只需译出意思,不必重复英文的近义词。例如"称心如意"只需翻译成 satisfactory,"胡言乱语"只需译成 talk nonsense,"发号施令"只需译成 issue orders,"粗制滥造"只需译成 crudely made,"惊天动地"只需译成 earth-shaking。

中译英时的省译更常见于旅游宣传文本,因为中文旅游文本的行文更具工整对偶、节奏铿锵的特色,显示出诗情画意,迎合中国游客的审美心理。而如前文所述,英文比较注重句子的构架严整,表达思维缜密,行文注重逻辑,用词强调简洁自然。所以,中文旅游文本的修辞省译成为一种必然。

◇ 例 18

徽派建筑是中国古建筑最重要的流派之一。徽派建筑构思精巧、自然得体、造型丰富，讲究韵律美，以马头墙、小青瓦最有特色；在建筑雕刻艺术的综合运用上，融石雕、木雕、砖雕为一体，显得富丽堂皇，极具文化气息。

Huizhou architecture style is one of the most important styles in ancient Chinese architecture. The architecture is designed in various shapes, characterized by Matou Walls and Chinese-style tiles.

◇ 例 19

上海是一座极具现代化而又不失中国传统特色的海派文化大都市，处处显现着她的独特魅力，现代与古典的完美融合，让人们无法抗拒。黄浦江游览一直是上海旅游中的一个传统旅游节目。乘坐在游船上，黄浦江两岸的更替交叠与华灯璀璨可谓尽收眼底。

Shanghai is a metropolis combining classical and modern elements, with its special features. The Huangpu River Tour is an unforgettable experience for visitors, who can have a full view of the changing lights and scenes along the river.

◇ 例 20

对于贵州人来说，吃一些时令野菜，用舌尖感受春的气息，也是春天的打开方式。比如蕨菜炒腊肉，便是许多贵州人春季一定要吃的心头好。

For Guizhou people, cooking some fresh wild vegetables is one of the means of celebrating the arrival of spring. For instance, the fried Chinese bacon with fiddlehead is a favorite dish of local people in this season.

◇ 例 21

四月份来贵州，安顺的油菜花田不能错过，层层叠叠的梯田上开满了黄灿灿的油菜花，无际的花海，美不胜收。

If you visit Guizhou in April, the sea of rape flowers on terraced fields in Anshun is a must-see.

仔细对照阅读例 18—21 的原文和译文，不难发现原文的下划线部分在英译文中多多少少都进行了省译，译文注重传达原文的实质信息，渲染的成分均低调处理，属于修辞省译。

翻译不仅是语言之间的转换，更是思维的转换。因此，翻译如果只是语言之间的转换，必定会出现翻译腔，必定会有一些译文不能被译语读者接受。对于修辞省译和增译，翻译学习者和翻译工作者一定要掌握中英文背后思维模式的差异，正如古人云：知己知彼，方能百战不殆。

拓展练习

翻译下列句子，请注意英译中时的修辞增译和中译英时的修辞省译。

1. If we have learnt one lesson during the past two years, it's that *flexibility*, *consistency*, mutual trust and creativity always pay off.
2. The golden trees and the enchanting atmosphere that surrounds Lake Gruyère makes this circular hike a *dreamy* experience.
3. Back at the car, the road trip continues on a *dreamy* route to the internationally famous St. Moritz where, *at the end of the day*, you will be able to appease your *hunger* with the many local specialities.
4. The road with its myriad of bridges, galleries and narrow tunnels meanders *through the rugged cliffs*—those who dare to venture further down can reach the bottom of the gorge via a staircase at the new visitors' centre.
5. Tens of thousands of years ago, glaciers created a fascinating landscape with a unique character that can be explored on various hikes, even in autumn. Alpine traditions are still alive in the valley and hikers are welcome guests in the alpine huts.
6. 外向型经济成为苏州经济的重要支柱，目前世界 500 强企业中已有 77 家来苏投资办厂，5 个国家级和 10 个省级开发区建设保持着良好的发展势头。
7. 一根细绳，一枚竹轮，轻轻提携便可轻舞旋转于高空，这种奇趣横生的运动即为抖空竹。

8. 你听说过东方威尼斯吗？它就是贵州的镇远古城，这里每一座建筑、每一块青砖石板都记载着历史遗迹，诉说着千年古镇的沧桑。城内古巷曲径通幽，春江渔火诗意盎然。

9. 暖春时节，黔东南从江县春意盎然，百花齐放，与侗寨独具特色的鼓楼、花桥、小溪交相辉映，让人沉醉。

10. 一场春雨后，贵州遵义市的龙山镇，在缥缈云雾中，就仿佛仙境一般，这样的春天，谁能不爱。

参考译文与简析

1. 过去两年我们获得的经验就是：灵活多变、协调一致、相互信任和富有创造力总会得到回报。(原文是在宣传自己的经验，中文需要体现宣传类文本的特点，将 flexibility 和 consistency 译成中文的"意复"短语"灵活多变"和"协调一致"，使宣传的文字更具美感。)

2. 金色的树木以及格吕耶尔湖畔迷人的氛围使这次环形徒步旅行成为一种如梦如幻的精彩体验。(原文是景点描写，为了更好地满足中文读者的审美思维，dreamy 译成了"如梦如幻"，"体验"前面增加了"精彩"。这些均属于修辞增译。)

3. 回到车内，继续沿如梦如幻的线路驶往举世闻名的圣莫里茨，一天精彩的游览结束时，饥肠辘辘的您将享用丰盛的当地特色美味。(原句的 dreamy 译成了"如梦如幻"，at the end of the day 译为"一天精彩的游览结束时"，hunger 译为"饥肠辘辘"，这些均属于修辞增译，符合中文对应文体的语体特点。)

4. 沿途经过无数桥梁、地下走廊和狭窄的隧道，蜿蜒穿过怪石嶙峋的峭壁。渴望进一步冒险的游客可以通过新游客中心的楼梯到达峡谷底部。(through the rugged cliffs 译成了"蜿蜒穿过怪石嶙峋的峭壁"，属于修辞增译。)

5. 数万年前，冰川创造了独具特色的迷人景观，即使在秋季，游客仍可以沿不同的徒步线路游览探索此地。山谷仍然保留着浓厚的阿尔卑斯山传统，高山小屋张开双臂热情欢迎徒步旅行的游客。(根据中文旅游类文体的特点，翻译时添加"浓厚""张开双臂"和"热情"等，属于修辞增译。)

6. Export-oriented economy is the pillar of local economy. So far 77 out of Fortune 500 businesses have set up their factories in Suzhou and ten provincial and five

national development zones are *gathering momentum*.（原文属于地方宣传，其中"重要"用来修饰"支柱"，符合中文背后的审美思维模式，但从语义上看显得冗余，因此省译。"保持着良好的发展势头"也做了适当的省译。这些都是修辞省译，旨在使译文符合英语读者的表达习惯。）

7. With a single string and a gentle toss, *the double-coned bamboo bobbin can spin in the air*. This unusual and interesting sport is known as diabolo spinning.（该句描写空竹，与中国文化密切相关，"轻轻提携便可轻舞旋转于高空"在译文中适当作了简化处理，符合英语的表达习惯，属于修辞省译。）

8. Have you ever heard of Venice of the East? Yes, it refers to the Zhenyuan Ancient Town in Guizhou. Here, each and every building, every brick and slab stone, carries the elements of history, *telling the stories of the millennium-old town. Lanes and paths wind their way*, with the idyllic atmosphere intensified by the river and lights on the fishing boats.（原文特别注重描写，符合中文背后的审美思维模式，但依照英文的表达习惯，"诉说着千年古镇的沧桑"和"城内古巷曲径通幽，春江渔火诗意盎然"均做了适当的简化处理，属于修辞省译。）

9. When spring comes to Congjiang County in Qiandongnan, *flowers bloom in the warm weather*. You will also be attracted by the Drum Tower, the Flower Bridge and streams in the villages of Dong ethnic group.（原句中"春意盎然""百花齐放"和"交相辉映"等词翻译时均作了适当的简化处理，属于修辞省译。）

10. Longshan Town in Zunyi City, Guizhou Province looks like *a wonderland veiled in the mist* after a spring drizzle. How can one resist the temptation of such beautiful scenery?（"在缥缈云雾中，就仿佛仙境一般"翻译时作了适当简化，属于修辞省译，符合英语表达习惯。）

第十六章　英文的替代和中文的重复

一般说来，英文常避免重复（作为修辞手段的重复除外），而使用替代手段来替代前文提到的词语或内容。中文则更倾向使用重复这一手法，特别是重复前文提到的人、事物和动作，如果使用替代手法，中文会显得意思不够明确，句式不够均衡。所以，在中英互译过程中，译者不可忽略这一区别，在翻译中要灵活处理。英译中的过程中大部分是将英文的不同代词转译为前文提到的名词，即译文中重复前文提到的名词。下面分别举例说明。

一、重复英文的人称代词所替代的名词

英文句子在后文中再提及前面的名词时，往往会使用代词，翻译成中文时，根据中文的习惯，往往重复代词所替代的名词。

◇ 例 1

He hated failure; he had conquered *it* all his life, risen above *it*, and despised *it* in others.

他讨厌失败，一生中曾战胜失败，超越失败，并且藐视他人的失败。

◇ 例 2

But Bell had boundless faith in the wisdom and dedication of Annie, and when *she* appealed to *him* for help, *he* dispatched his assistant, the venerable John Hitz, to investigate.

但贝尔对安妮的智慧和奉献精神充满无限的信心，因此，安妮向贝尔求助时，贝尔派自己的助手去调查此事，这位助手即可敬的约翰·希茨。

以上两个例句中，后面提及的代词在译文中变成了名词，即重复了代词所代替的名词，中文读起来才更顺畅，意思更加明确，否则不符合中文的表达习惯。

◇ 例 3

Bell's mind, and Helen's through his, responded to nature, too. Once, beneath an oak, *he* placed her hand on the trunk, and *she* felt the soft crepitation of raindrops on the leaves. For years after that *she* liked to touch trees in the rain. Then, on another day, *he* went with her to Niagara Falls and put her hand on the hotel windowpane so that *she* could sense the thunder of the river plunging over its shuddering escarpment.

贝尔的思想，以及贝尔通过自己的思想传递给海伦的思想，也对大自然做出了反应。一次，在一棵橡树下，贝尔把海伦的手放在树干上，海伦感觉到了雨滴落在树叶上发出的轻微噼啪声。此后多年，海伦一直喜欢在雨中抚摸树木。还有一天，贝尔和海伦一起去尼亚加拉大瀑布，贝尔把海伦的手放在酒店的窗玻璃上，这样海伦就能感觉到河流冲下颤抖的悬崖发出雷鸣般的响声。

原文的段落由多个句子构成。第一句话提到了 Bell 和 Hellen，其余的句子中均用代词来替代这两个人名，但在中文中，如果都译成"他"或"她"，句意会引起歧义，因此，后面的代词全部转译为名词。

◇ 例 4

Brill put up her hand and touched her fur. Dear little thing! It was nice to feel *it* again. She had taken *it* out of its box that afternoon, shaken out the moth-powder, given it a good brush, and rubbed the life back into the dim little eyes.

布里尔小姐抬手摸摸毛领，多么可爱的小东西啊，再次触摸它真好！她那天下午将毛领从盒子里取出，抖掉了防蛀粉，好好地梳理一番，将暗淡的小眼睛擦得又恢复了生气。

例 4 由四个句子组成，第三句和第四句中斜体的 it 均指前面提到的 fur，在第四句的译文中，将斜体的 it 还原成"毛领"，符合中文的表达习惯，如果直译为"它"，就显得有些拗口。

二、重复物主代词所代替的名词

英文中，物主代词是句内重要的衔接手段，翻译时物主代词有时需要省译，有时则要还原成物主代词所代表的名词，使译文明确具体。请看下面的例子。

◇ 例 5

Transtromer started writing poetry while studying at a Latin school in Stockholm. *His* work appeared in several journals before he published his first book of poetry, "*17 Poems*," in 1954.

特朗斯特罗姆在斯德哥尔摩一所拉丁学校上学期间就开始创作诗歌。第一本诗集《诗十七首》于1954年问世之前，特朗斯特罗姆的作品曾在几种期刊上发表。

◇ 例 6

In following *his* journey from that remote provincial railway station to his ancestral estates, once more I have been awe-struck by Tolstoy, the genius that produced so many masterpieces.

循着托尔斯泰的足迹，从偏远的乡村火车站到其祖先留下的庄园，我再一次对托尔斯泰这位创作了众多作品的天才肃然起敬。

◇ 例 7

This, as Bell pointed out, was the equivalent of the way a hearing child learned English. And it supported *his* long-standing emphasis on the use of the English language, rather than sign language, with deaf children.

正如贝尔指出，这相当于一个健听儿童学习英语的方式，也证实了贝尔长期以来的观点，他强调对聋儿说英语，而不用手语。

◆ 例 8

This has been our position—but not *theirs*.

这一直是我们的立场,而不是他们的<u>立场</u>。

很明显,以上四个例子中斜体部分的物主代词,如果直译或省译均会影响中文意思的通顺,翻译时需要重复它们所代表的名词,这样才能保证中译文符合中文的表达习惯。

三、重复关系代词所替代的名词

英语定语从句中的关系代词如果译成后置成分,一般需要还原该关系代词所代替的名词,这样才能使表达更明确和具体。请看下面的例子。

◆ 例 9

A friend of Keller's had spoken to Anagnos about Helen's case months earlier, perhaps at the instance of Helen's mother, *who* had read about Laura Bridgman in Charles Dickens' *American Notes*.

几个月前,凯勒的一位朋友就曾向阿纳格诺斯谈起过海伦的情况,也许是应海伦母亲的请求,因为<u>海伦的母亲</u>在查尔斯·狄更斯的《美国纪行》中读到了劳拉·布里奇曼的故事。

◆ 例 10

The sun did not shine clearly, but it spread through the clouds a tender, diffused light, crossed by level cloud-bars, *which* stretched to a great length, quite parallel.

阳光并不十分明媚,但透过云层柔和地弥散开来,穿过水平的条状云彩,<u>这些云彩</u>伸向远方,仿佛一条条平行线。

◆ 例 11

The tints in the sky were wonderful, every conceivable shade of blue-grey, *which* contrived to modulate into the golden brilliance in which the sun was veiled.

空中的色彩美妙绝伦，呈各种不同的蓝灰色，这些蓝灰色竭力幻化成一片金色光辉，给太阳蒙上了面纱。

以上三个例子原文中斜体的关系代词引导的定语从句都是非限定性定语从句，起到补充说明的作用，翻译时无法译成前置的定语，后置时重复一下斜体的关系代词所代表的名词，这样译文才能更符合中文的表达习惯，意思更清晰具体。

四、重复不定代词所替代的名词

英文中有些不定代词（如 some、any 和 others）在句子中替代前面提及的名词，翻译时需重复所替代的名词。请看下面的例子。

◇ 例 12

Our most original compositions are composed exclusively of expressions derived from *others*.

我们最初的作品完全是用源自别人作品中的表达方式写成的。

◇ 例 13

Some countries have joined the organization and still *some* are hesitating.

一些国家加入了该组织，还有些国家在犹豫不决。

◇ 例 14

If you need any money, you have to get some out of the bank; there is hardly *any* in the house.

如果你需要钱，就得去银行取，家里几乎没有钱了。

上面三个例子中，例 12 中的 others 即 other compositions，例 13 中的 some 即 some countries，例 14 中的 any 即 any money。这些不定代词在译文中如果不重复所替代的名词，就会显得拗口，翻译时需要重复所替代的名词，这样意思表达更明确和具体。

当然，英文除了上述替代方式，还有其他替代方式，翻译时也需要灵活处理，看中译文是否要根据表达习惯进行重复。

✧ 例 15

Even today, many otherwise educated men—like those savages who can count to three but lump together all numbers beyond four—cannot grasp the profound distinction between solar and stellar space. *The first* is the space enclosing our neighboring worlds, the planets; *the second* is that which embraces those distant suns, the stars, and it is literally millions of times greater.

即使在今天，就像弄不清4以上数字的未开化原始人一样，很多以其他方式接受教育的人也无法理解太阳系空间与星际空间之间的巨大差异。太阳系空间是我们附近的空间，由行星组成；星际空间则是由遥远的恒星组成的空间，要比太阳系空间大数百万倍。

该例中，the first 和 the second 指前文提到的 the solar and stellar space，如果直接译为"第一个"和"第二个"，意思会不清晰，因此，译文中重复了所指代的名词，这样意思就清楚多了。

通过以上举例分析，我们就可以知道中英文在替代和重复方面的区别，以后翻译时要注意替代和重复方面的转换，从而使译文更清晰。

拓展练习

翻译下列句子，请注意英译中时的替代转译为重复。

1. The river-channel could be discerned only by the boiling of the current. *It* had risen above the crown of the main stone arch, and swirled and plunged underneath it.
2. This might be one definition of a classic: as much as we read *it*, *it* reads us.
3. Now and then Bell thought about Helen's future course in life. As *she* made *her* way through college *he* began to feel that "with her gifts of mind and imagination there should be a great future open to her in literature."

4. This book contained accounts of Helen's education by Annie Sullivan and others, among them Sarah Fuller, *who* had recently given Helen her first lessons in speech.

5. There were few roads visible below, most transportation in Nepal being by foot along ancient trails *that* connect and bind the country together.

6. Alexandra's life is dedicated purely to skiing. She grew up at Lake Schwarzsee in Fribourg and started off as a ski racer. Later, she became a snow sports instructor, gaining a federal professional certificate. Now, as an expert at Swiss Snowsports, she trains future ski instructors. Alexandra also works as a ski instructor in Zermatt.

7. Salinger found Hemingway to be utterly unlike the rough, tough, brusque, outdoors, literary lion he was expecting and shyly mentioned to *him* a story *Slight Rebellion in Manhattan*, which he had written in 1941 and offered to *The New Yorker*.

8. Gates reveals that his interest in philanthropy comes in part from his parents, *who* both set an example for him as a child.

9. *Ours* is not a time of self-esteem or self-confidence—as was, for instance, the nineteenth century, when self-esteem may be seen oozing from its portraits.

10. But with his father determined that *he* should not be an actor, and his mother, as *he* saw it, overprotective, in 1934 Salinger entered Valley Forge Military Academy, Pennsylvania. He spent two years there, graduating in 1936. While there *he* edited the academy's yearbook *Crossed Sabres*. More important, in this robust and not wholly congenial ambience he began writing short stories.

参考译文与简析

1. 只有在湍急的水流中才能辨清河道,<u>水流</u>已上升到主石拱的顶部,接着打着旋涡,又从底部一泻而过。(英文第二句中的主语 it 指前一句最后一个单词 current,翻译时最好不要译成"它",而是重复 current 的中文"水流",这样意思更清晰。翻译时,两个句子可以融合翻译,译为一句话。)

2. 这可能是经典作品的一种定义:我们阅读<u>经典</u>多少,<u>经典</u>就阅读我们多少。(原文后面两个代词 it 均转译为名词"经典"。)

3. 贝尔不时会考虑海伦未来的人生道路。<u>海伦</u>大学毕业时,贝尔开始觉得"凭借注意力和想象力方面的天赋,她在文学领域应该有一个辉煌的未来。"(原文第二句使用了多个代词，翻译时需要适当转译为名词，使句意更清晰。）

4. 这本书包含了安妮·莎莉文和莎拉·富勒等人对海伦进行教育的描述。富勒在会前的一段时间给海伦上了其生平第一堂有声课。（关系代词 who 在译文中根据上下文转译为名词"莎拉·富勒"。）

5. 下面看不到几条路，尼泊尔的交通大多是在古老的小道上步行，<u>这些小道</u>将全国各地连在了一起。（关系代词 that 译成名词"这些小道"。）

6. 亚历山德拉纯粹是为滑雪而生。她在弗里堡的施瓦尔茨湖畔长大，最初是一名滑雪运动员，后来成为一名雪上运动教练，获得了瑞士联邦专业证书。现在，亚历山德拉作为瑞士滑雪运动专家对未来的滑雪教练进行培训，还在采尔马特担任滑雪教练。（第三句中的 she 译成了名词"亚历山德拉"。）

7. 塞林格发现，海明威完全不是他想象中粗俗、粗暴、粗鲁、粗野的文学"雄狮"形象。塞林格胆怯地和<u>海明威</u>谈到了自己的短篇小说《冲出曼哈顿的轻度反叛》，该小说创作于 1941 年并向《纽约客》投稿。（原句中代词太多，应根据需要将代词转译为名词，him 还原成"海明威"，否则代词太多不知所指。）

8. 盖茨表示，自己对慈善事业的兴趣，部分得益于父母的影响，因为<u>父母</u>在盖茨年幼时就为他树立了好的榜样。（原文的关系代词 who 在译文中转译为"父母"。）

9. <u>我们的时代</u>并不是一个自尊或者自信的时代，比如说不像 19 世纪，从那个时代的人物肖像中就可以看到流溢而出的自尊。（根据句意可以推断出句首的 ours 指 our time，因此翻译成名词短语"我们的时代"。）

10. 由于父亲坚持不让<u>塞林格</u>成为演员，<u>塞林格</u>自己又觉得母亲过分溺爱自己，于是 1934 年塞林格进入宾夕法尼亚州的瓦莱弗格军事学校，在那里待了两年，1936 年毕业。在此期间，<u>塞林格</u>编纂了学院的年鉴《十字军刀》。更重要的是，在这种充满活力但并不十分宜人的氛围中，他开始创作短篇小说。（这一段话中的代词很多，但中译文根据中文表达习惯，多处将代词转译为名词，即"塞林格"。）

第十七章　中文重复名词和动词的翻译

中文句子和篇章重复使用一些名词或动词可以使意思更加清晰，使语气更加平衡，同时还可以增强表达的节奏感。根据前一章分析的英文替代特点，中文的很多重复在英译文中一般都用替代的方法处理。下面具体分析中文名词和动词的重复现象及其翻译。

一、名词重复及其翻译

在中文里，即使前面已经使用了某一名词，再提及这一名词时往往仍然使用实称，即重复该名词或名词的一部分，这样会使意思更加清晰，如果使用替代，反而会让行文读起来不通顺或不明确。但是，通过前一章对英文的分析，我们知道，英文不倾向使用名词重复，反而通常使用替代（尤其是代词）来完成句子或语篇的衔接。那么，中文重复的名词在翻译时一般转换为代词。请看下面的例子。

◇ 例 1

但是韩馥仍然忧虑惊恐，请求袁绍让他离去，<u>袁绍</u>同意，于是<u>韩馥</u>就去投奔陈留郡太守张邈。

However, Han Fu, still worried and frightened, asked Yuan Shao to let him leave, to which *the latter* agreed, so *he* went to join Zhang Miao, magistrate of Chenliu.

◇ 例 2

一定的文化是一定社会的政治和经济的反映，又给予<u>一定社会的政治和经济</u>以巨大的作用和影响。

Any given culture is a reflection of the politics and economy of a given society, and the former in turn has a tremendous effect and influence on *the latter*.

◇ 例 3

房客的家属们哭着，诉说着，向着我的祖父跪了下来，于是祖父把两匹棕色的马从车上解下来还了回去。

The tenant's family members, weeping and pleading, knelt down to my grandfather, *who* then untied two brown horses and returned them.

◇ 例 4

1985 年以后，中国政府就开始注重推动科技计划，因为科技计划是高科技经济增长、经济转型和国家独立的主要推动力量。

Science and technology programs have been promoted by the Chinese government since 1985 because *they* are key engines of economic growth based on high technology, economic transformation, and national independence.

以上例子中，下划线的部分都是句子中重复的名词，英译文根据情况使用了人称代词、关系代词和 the latter 等形式进行替代，这些替代都是英文句子内部衔接的方式，符合英语的表达习惯。

另外，中文的重复不仅表现在同一个句子当中，相邻的一句话也会重复使用前面的名词。而英文往往使用替代，尤其是代词替代。请看下面的例子。

◇ 例 5

729 年，李白因喝醉酒误撞地方官员李长史的车马，被官府传讯。由于认错态度诚恳，李长史放了李白一马，没有处罚他。

Once in 729, Li Bai was summoned by the local court, because when drunk, he had blocked the way of the local official Mr. Li, who was being carried in his chariot. Thanks to his sincere apology, *he* was forgiven rather than punished.

◇ 例 6

然而，在保持生态环境问题上，发展中国家存在的问题较为严重。特别是，一些发展中国家或没有认识到可持续发展的深刻内涵，或认识得很不深刻，采取的措施也不得力。

However, as for environmental protection, there exist serious problems in developing countries. Especially, some of *them* have failed to take effective measures due to their ignorance or insufficient understanding of the significance of sustainable development.

◇ 例 7

1900年10月冰心出生于福建福州，1901年其全家迁至上海。幸运的是，冰心有鼓励她学习和写作的父母。

Bing Xin was born in Fuzhou, Fujian Province in October 1900, and *she* was brought in 1901 to Shanghai by his parents, *who* encouraged *her* to read and write.

以上三个例子中，"李白""发展中国家"和"冰心"都是重复前一句中的名词，翻译时没有重复翻译，而是使用人称代词和关系代词等替代，符合英语的表达习惯。

◇ 例 8

有的问题是教科书上的，有的问题是教科书外的。有的问题向老师提出来，老师给予满意的答复，有的问题山桃儿就攒了下来。

Some questions were about what she had learned from her textbooks while *others* were not. *Some* were raised to her teacher, *who* gave satisfactory answers while *others* were kept to herself.

这个例子中原文重复的名词不仅表现在句内，还表现在下一句，重复比较多，是中文叙述类文本的特点。英译文如果重复出现某一名词，就会使句内和句际衔接不顺畅。中文中重复性名词翻译时均使用替代，以符合英文的表达习惯。

除重复完整的名词外，中文有时还重复部分名词，即后文提及前文提到的名词时，往往使用"这""该""这些"等指示代词加上前面的中心名词，来表示前面已经提到的名词。请看下面的例子。

◇ 例 9

由于对新产品和新程序的开发和改进提供资金支持，"863 计划"直接提高了中国企业的创新竞争力。另外，<u>该计划</u>帮助企业更为迅速地将新技术推向市场。

The "863 Program" has directly contributed to the innovative competitiveness of Chinese corporations thanks to the financial support it offers for the creation or adaptation of new products and processes. In addition, *it* helps companies put new technologies on the market more quickly.

◇ 例 10

2000 年，中关村科技园的管理部门建立了第一批风险投资公司，旨在支持研究机构成立的中小型高科技公司，并推动<u>这些公司</u>的发展，提高其竞争力。

In 2000 Zhongguancun Science Park (ZSP) authorities set up the first venture capital companies aiming at supporting small and medium-sized high-tech companies established by research institutes and helping *them* grow and be more competitive.

不难看出，例 9 中的"该计划"重复了部分前文的"863 计划"，例 10 中的"这些公司"部分重复了前文的"中小型高科技公司"。但在英译文中，这些重复性名词均可以转译为代词，以显示出英文以替代为衔接手段的特征。

二、动词重复及其翻译

中文的重复不仅表现在名词，还表现在动词上。因此，翻译中文重复性动词，一般也使用替代或省译的办法，不必重复动词。

◇ 例 11

在中国经营的美国公司必须了解和理解中国文化，中国公司在海外经营也要了解和理解外国文化。

American companies doing business in China must learn about and understand Chinese culture. *The same* applies to Chinese companies when they do business overseas.

◇ 例 12

人类的种种技术，都是人的延伸，比如汽车是人腿的延伸，电脑是人脑的延伸。

Technologies invented by human beings are extensions of themselves. For example, the car is the extension of human's leg and the computer, *that* of human's brain.

◇ 例 13

信中，李白不仅表现得诚惶诚恐，还把李长史比作"庄公"，把自己比作"螳螂"。

In the letter, Li Bai showed his uneasiness while comparing the official Mr. Li to Duke Zhuang of the Qi State in the Spring and Autumn Period, who was said to admire talent, and himself *to* a mantis, the insect which hindered the duke's chariot in a fable.

上述例子中，下划线部分的动词在前面均出现过一次，例 11 的"了解和理解外国文化"在译文中用 the same 替代，英文的意思依然明确。试想，如果每句话中的重复动词都重复翻译，势必使英文读者感到冗长。

综上所述，我们可以看出，中文是一种重复性语言。一般来说，如果直接把中文重复的部分翻译出来，会使译文显得晦涩、牵强。所以，中译英时，大多数情况下会将重复手段转译为替代手段，有时为了行文的简洁也可进行省译。因此，翻译学习者要领会两种语言的不同，并根据目的语的表达习惯进行翻译，这样才能使译文流畅。

拓展练习

翻译下列句子，请注意中文重复部分的翻译。

1. 压力和焦虑会导致失眠，同时<u>失眠</u>又反过来加剧紧张和焦虑。
2. 向裴长史求职被拒后，李白离开安陆，去了长安。可在<u>长安</u>待了一年多，却处处碰壁，最后只好吟着《行路难》扫兴而归。
3. 山桃儿不好意思总是那么问老师问老师的，因为自己连一顿谢师饭也没有请<u>老师</u>吃过。
4. 当然，对于茶馆而言，最重要的文化自然应该是茶文化，而茶文化最直接的表现形式应该首推茶艺，所以，几乎所有的茶馆都在创造、创新着自己的<u>茶艺</u>。
5. 青蛇精在深山中修炼，习武多年，终于砸烂了那座塔，救出白蛇精。至此，<u>白蛇精</u>与丈夫、儿子又得团聚。
6. 旧的模型可以被新的观测或者实验所推翻或者修改，但是这些<u>旧的模型</u>也都是科学理论，是追求"唯一"正确的科学理论的历程中必须经过的阶段。
7. 我等着要上路，越<u>等</u>越不耐烦，哪里是<u>等</u>一会儿，一<u>等</u>就是老半天。
8. 我们支持你的工作，也支持他的<u>工作</u>。
9. 在中国农历二十四节气中，既是节气又是节日的只有清明。但是，<u>清明</u>作为节日，与纯粹的节气又有所不同，它包含着丰富的风俗活动内容。
10. 风筝分为硬翅和软翅两种。<u>硬翅</u>风筝骨架不能拆卸，受风力强；<u>软翅</u>风筝骨架可以拆卸装盒，便于保存和携带。

参考译文与简析

1. Pressure and anxiety lead to insomnia, *which*, in return, intensifies tension and anxiety.（原句中"失眠"出现了两次，翻译时根据英文的衔接方式，将后半句译为非限定性定语从句，关系代词 which 指代"失眠"。）
2. After being refused by the official Mr. Pei, Li Bai left Anlu for Chang'an. He stayed *there* for more than one year and then returned frustrated composing his poem *A Hard Journey* on his way.（译文中用副词 there 指代原文中重复出现的"长安"。）
3. Shantao found it embarrassing to keep asking her teacher questions since she had not invited *him* to a thank-you dinner yet.（原文中"老师"重复使用多次，后面

提及的几处在译文中均用代词指代。)

4. Since the most important culture of a teahouse should be the tea culture embodied first by the art of tea making, *which* is created and innovated by almost every teahouse. (原句中的"茶文化"和"茶艺"均重复使用,英译文中第二个"茶文化"省译,第二个"茶艺"使用关系代词指代。)

5. The Green Snake, after practicing martial art in the mountains for years, succeeded in smashing the tower and rescued the White Snake, *who* was eventually able to reunite with her husband and her son. (原句第二句中的"白蛇精"使用了关系代词来指代。)

6. Old models can be overthrown or modified by new observations or experiments, but *they* remain scientific theories and the must-stage in the pursuit of the "only" right scientific theory. (原句中第二次出现的"旧的模型"在译文中用代词 they 来指代。)

7. I *waited* with growing impatience to get on my way, not for one minute but for quite a considerable time. (原句中动词"等"重复了多次,译文中 waited 仅使用了一次,其他均省译。)

8. We will *support* both your and his work. (原句中用了两个"支持",译文中没有重复。)

9. Among the twenty-four solar terms on the Chinese lunar calendar, Qingming is the only one to be both a solar term and a festival. A diversity of cultural activities are held *on that day*. (原文中"清明"重复了一次,但英译文中用 on that day 来替代。)

10. Kites are divided into "hard-winged" and "soft-winged" ones. *The former*'s frame cannot be disassembled and they are highly wind-resistant, whereas *the latter's* frame may be disassembled and they can be placed in a box, making them easy to store and portable. (原文"风筝"重复了两次,译文使用了 the former 和 the latter 来替代,使表达更简洁,符合英语的表达习惯。)

第十八章　英文长句的翻译

英文句子的长度约为15~17个单词，句子如果超出30个单词就会显得冗长复杂。英文的长句可以定义为由多个主谓结构或多个修饰成分（包括定语和状语）组成的句子。关于长句的译法，不少翻译教材都提到过。比如张培基在《英汉翻译教程》中将英语长句翻译归为四种，即顺序法、逆序法、分译法和综合法。实际上，这些方法是将译文与原文对比的一种描述，也就是对翻译结果的描述。译者开始翻译长句的时候，并不知道如何翻译整个句子，而是经过一定的分析，然后根据中文的表达习惯将信息进行一定的重组，得出译文。具体说来，长句的翻译首先要分析整个句子的主干，再分析其他成分，理清各部分之间的逻辑关系，分析过程中还要将分析出来的信息转换为中文放在脑子里，然后用通顺的中文将分析出的逻辑关系和原句的意思表达出来。所以，英文长句的翻译均基于对原文的分析和中文的重新组织，这种分析和重组可以称为"层层剥笋"的方法。换言之，英语长句的翻译离不开"分析—转换—重组"的过程。下面举例分析英语长句的翻译。

◆ 例1

At the Perkins Institution a solemn committee (Mark Twain in his outrage called it "a collection of decayed human turnips") cross-questioned the bewildered and frightened child at great length with Annie Sullivan sent out of the room, before concluding that Helen had unwittingly summoned up the story from her remarkable memory rather than from her imagination as she supposed.

该句各部分的分析和译文如下：

（1）句子的主结构：a solemn committee cross-questioned the bewildered and frightened child（装腔作势的委员会对这个充满困惑和惊恐的孩子进行了长时间盘问）

（2）状语：with Annie Sullivan sent out of the room（将安妮·莎莉文赶出房间）

（3）时间状语：before concluding that Helen had unwittingly summoned up the story from her remarkable memory rather than from her imagination as she supposed（在得出结论之前，结论是：海伦不知不觉地从自己非凡的记忆中提取了这个故事，而非她自己认为的那样：是自己想象出来的）

（4）地点状语：At the Perkins Institution（在帕金斯盲人学校）

经过以上分析，我们基本理清了原文的逻辑关系，而且分析过程中也将每一部分的信息转换成中文存在脑子里，即上述分析括号内的部分。最后，将这些信息在保留原文逻辑关系的前提下（注意不是保留原文的形式），根据中文的表达将以上转换来的中文进行重新组合。当然，上述分析中的（3）不要保留"在得出结论之前"，其实际意思就是"之后得出结论"。原文中关于马克·吐温的观点在译文中也可以放在括号内。这样一来，就可以得到下面的译文：

在帕金斯盲人学校，装腔作势的委员会（马克·吐温愤怒地将其称为"一堆腐烂的人形萝卜"）将安妮·莎莉文赶出房间，对海伦这个充满困惑和惊恐的孩子进行了长时间盘问，然后得出结论，海伦不知不觉地从自己非凡的记忆中提取了这个故事，而非她自己认为的那样：是自己想象出来的。

◇ 例2

Yet, foreign and domestic policies proceed about as always, with only sporadic recognition that control of territory has become an uncertain and ambiguous concept, that freedom of national action and inviolability of borders have long since lost so much of their traditional meaning, that the size of the resources of most nation-states are incommensurate with the requirements of modern technology, and that international organizations must fill a more important role than simply amplify big power goals.

该句各部分的分析和译文如下:

(1) 句子的主结构: foreign and domestic policies proceed about as always (外交政策和国内政策一如既往地推行)

(2) 状语: with only sporadic recognition (只是人们偶尔会认识到)

(3) recognition 后面第一个同位语: that control of territory has become an uncertain and ambiguous concept (对领土的控制已经成为不确定和模糊的概念)

(4) recognition 后面第二个同位语: that freedom of national action and inviolability of borders have long since lost so much of their traditional meaning (国家行动自由和边界不可侵犯早已失去了传统意义)

(5) recognition 后面第三个同位语: that the size of the resources of most nation-states are incommensurate with the requirements of modern technology (大多数民族国家的资源规模与现代技术要求不相称)

(6) recognition 后面第四个同位语: that international organizations must fill a more important role than simply amplify big power goals (国际组织必须发挥更重要的作用,而不仅仅是放大大国的目标)

经过以上分析和各部分的翻译,我们基本理清了原文的逻辑关系和主要信息。尤其是四个同位语从句前面的 recognition 动作性很强,根据前面讲过的内容,我们知道这个词最好转译为"意识到",从句的内容可以放在后面作它的宾语。这样一来,例2的译文如下:

然而,外交政策和国内政策一如既往地推行,只是人们偶尔会认识到:对领土的控制已经成为不确定和模糊的概念,国家行动自由和边界不可侵犯早已失去了传统意义,大多数民族国家的资源规模与现代技术要求不相称,国际组织必须发挥更重要的作用,而不仅仅是放大大国的目标。

◇ 例 3

Isabella, who had been treated by Hippolita like a daughter, and who returned that tenderness with equal duty and affection, was scarcely less assiduous about the princess, at the same time endeavouring to partake and lessen the weight of sorrow which she saw Matilda strove to suppress, for whom she had conceived the warmest sympathy of friendship.

该句各部分的分析和译文如下：

（1）句子的主干：Isabella...was scarcely less assiduous about the princess（伊莎贝拉也同样关注公主玛蒂尔达）

（2）主干的主语后面跟的非限定性定语从句：who had been treated by Hippolita like a daughter, and who returned that tenderness with equal duty and affection（被希波莉塔当作女儿一样对待，用同样的责任和爱意温柔地去回报）（后一部分的意思是像女儿一样去照顾希波莉塔）

（3）句子主干后面是现在分词短语：at the same time endeavouring to partake and lessen the weight of sorrow...（同时努力分担和减轻那份痛苦）

（4）sorrow 后面的定语从句：which she saw Matilda strove to suppress（伊莎贝拉看到玛蒂尔达试图去控制的……）

（5）修饰 Matilda 的定语从句：for whom she had conceived the warmest sympathy of friendship（她对玛蒂尔达抱有最温暖而友好的同情）

经过上述分析，原文的逻辑关系以及意思已经非常明确，可以根据这一分析对转换出来的中文进行重组与润色，尤其是要考虑到这一长句所在的文学文体，得到如下译文：

希波莉塔平素一直把伊莎贝拉当作自己的女儿疼爱，所以此时的伊莎贝拉也像女儿一样竭力照顾公爵夫人。同时，伊莎贝拉也很关心玛蒂尔达，尽力分担并减轻她的痛苦，因为她对玛蒂尔达抱有最温暖而友好的同情。

◇ 例 4

Attempts to suppress basic science are surely unwise and futile. They are unwise because of the penalties paid in the imposition of intellectual control that would be required; unwise because the agreements necessary with other countries to avoid the danger of scientific surprise would be unenforceable except under conditions of extreme and unrealistic intellectual control, and unwise because such a ban would mean forgoing highly desirable technological applications—including some which might ameliorate technology—that arise from scientific discoveries.

该例包含两句话，第二句显然是一个长句，但这个长句中的主结构很简单，即 They are unwise，其中 they 指的是前文提到的 attempts。第二句主结构之后都是说明这些企图不明智的原因。第一个原因是介词短语，但里面有一个定语从句 that would be required 修饰 intellectual control，这个定语从句较短，可以译为中文的定语。最后一个原因状语从句需要分析一下，即 such a ban would mean forgoing highly desirable technological applications 是主要部分，that arise from scientific discoveries 是定语从句，修饰 applications，这一部分可以直接译为定语，放在被修饰词的前面。破折号部分 which might ameliorate technology 修饰 some，some 指代 some applications，即"部分可以使技术得到改进的应用"。这一部分重组时最好放在最后，而不是像原文那样使用两个破折号，因为这不符合中文的习惯。经过分析，我们就可以得到例4的译文：

企图控制基础科学，显然不明智而且徒劳。之所以不明智，是因为实施必要的知识控制需要付出代价；之所以不明智，是因为除非实施极端和不现实的知识控制，否则无法执行有必要与其他国家达成有关避免科学意外危险的协议；之所以不明智，还因为这种禁令意味着放弃来源于科学发现的优良技术应用，包括部分可以使技术得到改进的应用。

◇ 例 5

I speak, I'm sure, for the faculty of the liberal arts college and for the faculties of the specialized schools as well, when I say that a university has no real existence and no real purpose except as it succeeds in putting you in touch, both as specialists and as humans, with those human minds your human mind needs to include.

该句各部分的分析和译文如下：

（1）句子的主干：I speak for the faculty of the liberal arts college and for the faculties of the specialized schools as well（我道出了文科学院全体教师以及专业学院全体教师的心声）

（2）插入语：I'm sure（我坚信）

（3）时间状语从句：when I say that a university has no real existence and no real purpose except as it succeeds in putting you in touch, both as specialists and as humans, with those human minds your human mind needs to include（当我说大学就不会真正存在，也没有真正的目的，除它成功地使作为专修某一专业的你们和作为人类的你们接触到你们的思想需要纳入的这些人类思想外）这个状语从句中带了一个宾语从句 a university has no real existence and no real purpose except as it succeeds in putting you in touch, both as specialists and as humans, with those human minds your human mind needs to include，宾语从句中又有一个 except 从句。

基于以上分析，再根据中文将条件和时间状语放在前面的表达习惯，将以上转换来的中文重新组合，得到如下译文：

如果一所大学没有成功地使作为专修某一专业的你们和作为人类的你们接触到你们的思想需要纳入的这些人类思想，那么这所大学就不算真正的大学，也没有真正的目的。我这样说的时候，坚信自己道出了文科学院全体教师以及专业学院全体教师的心声。

法律文体中常用长句，译者更要认真分析原文，理清关系。请看下面的例子。

◇ **例 6**

Either Party may terminate the contract in case of failure on the part of the other Party to fulfill or perform any of its obligations hereunder and in the event that such failure remains unremedied sixty (60) days after the service of a written notice as described in Article X below by the non-defaulting Party to the other Party specifying the failure in question and requiring it to be remedied.

该句各部分的分析和译文如下：
（1）主结构：Either Party may terminate the contract（一方可终止本合同）
（2）两个条件成分：in case of failure on the part of the other Party to fulfill or perform any of its obligations hereunder（如果一方未履行其本合同规定的任何

义务）和 in the event that such failure remains unremedied sixty (60) days（六十日内，其仍未予以改正）

（3）时间状语：after the service of a written notice as described in Article X below by the non-defaulting Party to the other Party specifying the failure in question and requiring it to be remedied（按照下述第 X 条规定在另一方向其送达书面通知指出其违约行为并要求其予以改正后）

根据上述分析和每一部分的翻译，我们需要对中文进行重组，得到的译文如下：

如果一方未履行其本合同规定的任何义务，而且按照下述第 X 条规定在另一方向其送达书面通知指出其违约行为并要求其予以改正后六十(60)日内，其仍未予以改正，另一方则可终止本合同。

总之，由于英文有很多修饰成分，短语多，从句多，在句法结构上可以层层修饰，因此长句比较常见。翻译长句时，必须对英文句子各部分之间的语法关系进行分析，厘清其中的逻辑关系，一边分析一边将各部分转换成中文，然后再根据汉语的表达习惯进行重组。中文的表达顺序有的与原文顺序相同，有的大相径庭。可以说，英语长句的翻译要根据汉语的表达习惯进行调整，使译文更符合中文读者的预期。

拓展练习

翻译下列句子，请注意英文长句的分析和翻译。

1. If, in fact, gigantic new particle accelerators may make it possible to obtain the knowledge that would make such a reaction suitable for military use, the layman is asking a legitimate question when he wonders whether he wants his government to spend the money to bring that possibility about.

2. The possibility of sudden developments that would make a new weapons system feasible, such as an effective missile defense or a discovery that reduces the cost and complexity of powerful weapons, thereby making them available to smaller

countries, are cases in point.

3. Assuming any resolution of the limitations of sovereignty other than a simple division of the entire oceans among coastal states (which is most unlikely, since it would not conform with present political realities: Russia would get little, Britain, a new empire based on her island possessions), some kind of regime will have to be established for unassigned areas.

4. Whether the existing convention remains in force, or some modification is eventually agreed to (the U.S. has proposed international ownership beyond 200 meters), one can hypothesize the kind of international functions that may have to be performed if private or public interests are to be able to exploit the resources of the seabed with relative security of investment, and if demands for equitable distribution of benefits are to be satisfied.

5. But many thought Transtromer's nationality stood in the way of receiving the prestigious, $1.5 million Nobel from the Swedish Academy, which has often been accused of bias in favor of literature from mainland Europe.

6. Thus we have the need for DDT for health and food, but also its potentially catastrophic effects on animal life; the need for fertilizer to produce adequate amounts of food, but also its effects on the eutrophication of bodies of water; the atmospheric effects of industrial effluents; the dangers of large-scale oil-spills arising from the transport of needed fuel in huge tankers; the radiation, waste-disposal and security problems associated with nuclear power plants.

7. Without doubt, the world will face the question of control or suppression of technology increasingly in the future, perhaps with regard to developments even more frightening than nuclear weapons in their power to influence the global environment or human heredity.

8. Technology will spread, will increase the dependence of one country on another, will create wholly new international relationships, will force new degrees of cooperation and dispute, will result in new threats to international stability, and will raise more problems of overpopulation and environmental pollution.

9. The role of Turkish-Cypriot women also, as demonstrated in the emerging

movement within the Turkish-Cypriot community in support of the efforts for reconciliation and the finding of a federal solution to the Cyprus problem, in particular in the last 15 months, has been very important as regards the efforts for a solution that would reunify the island and lead to peace and prosperity for its entire people.

10. The failure to insist upon the strict performance of any of these agreements, terms, covenants or conditions hereof shall not be deemed a waiver of any rights or remedies that either party hereto may have or a waiver of any subsequent breach or default in any of such agreements, terms, covenants and conditions.

参考译文与简析

1. 实际上，如果规模巨大的新粒子加速器使人们获得了一定的知识，能够使这种反应适用于军事用途，那么，外行人想知道自己是否希望政府花钱来实现这种可能，就会提出一个合理的问题。（这句话的主句是 the layman is asking a legitimate question when he wonders whether he wants his government to spend the money to bring that possibility about，其中又包含 when 引导的状语从句，状语从句包含 whether 引导的宾语从句。翻译时可以先翻译 when 引导的部分。前面 if 引导的状语从句译文中依然放在前面。）

2. 突如其来的技术发展可能会使新武器系统变得可行，例如有效导弹防御或发现可以降低强大武器的成本和复杂性，从而使小国也能使用这些武器。这些都是需要考虑的问题。（这句话的主结构是 The possibility...are cases in point，中间部分很长，是因为 developments 后面加了定语从句。翻译时需要一层层分析，然后再根据中文表达习惯进行组织。）

3. 假定采用主权限制的解决方案而非在沿海国家之间简单划分整个海洋（这几乎不可能，因为不符合目前的政治现实：如果这样，俄罗斯只能得到一点点海洋，而英国会成为一个新的帝国，因为拥有众多岛屿），就必须为未分配的地区建立某种制度。（这句话长在括号内的定语从句，但这一定语从句在译文中也可使用括号，括号前后译文可以按照原文顺序排列。）

4. 无论现存公约继续有效，还是最终达成某种一致的修改意见（美国已建议深度超过 200 米的区域所有权归国际公有），如果私人利益集团或公共利益集团能够在投资相对安全的情况下开发海底资源，如果可以满足公平分配利益需求，那么就要设定必须履行的某种国际职能。（这句话的主结构是 one can hypothesize the kind of international functions that may have to be performed，主结构后面是条件状语 if private or public interests are to be able to exploit the resources of the seabed with relative security of investment, and if demands for equitable distribution of benefits are to be satisfied，这一并列的条件状语在译文中提到主结构的前面。原文最前面的部分在译文中的顺序保持不变。）

5. 但很多人认为，国籍是特朗斯特罗姆的绊脚石，阻碍了他从瑞典文学院获得著名的诺贝尔文学奖，赢得150万美元的奖金。人们经常抱怨瑞典文学院更垂青欧洲大陆的文学作品。（原文最后的定语从句起补充说明作用，可以放在译文的最后单独成句。）

6. 因此，我们因为健康和食物而需要DDT杀虫剂，但也要考虑DDT杀虫剂对动物生命潜在的灾难性影响；我们需要化肥来生产足够数量的食物，但也要考虑化肥对水体富营养化的影响；此外，还要考虑工业废水对大气的影响、大型油轮所需燃料运输产生的大规模石油泄漏危险以及核电站辐射、废物处理和安全问题等。（这句话原文虽然很长，但是原文用分号隔开，中文也可使用分号。每一部分的逻辑并不十分复杂，翻译起来也不算难。）

7. 毫无疑问，世界未来将越来越多地面临管控或压制技术的问题，也许在影响全球环境或人类遗传能力方面，技术发展甚至比核武器更令人恐惧。（该句原文主结构是 the world will face the question of control or suppression of technology increasingly in the future，后面 perhaps with regard to developments even more frightening than nuclear weapons in their power to influence the global environment or human heredity 虽然是个短语，但是结构比较复杂，需要分析一下。整体结构在译文中没有太大变化。）

8. 技术会传播，会增加一个国家对另一个国家的依赖，会创造全新的国际关系，会使合作和争端发展至新的阶段，会对国际稳定产生新的威胁，会引起更多人口过剩和环境污染问题。（该句有多个谓语动词并列，即 will spread、will increasethe dependence of one country on another、will create wholly new international relationships、will force new degrees of cooperation and dispute、will result in new threats to international stability 和 will raise more problems of

overpopulation and environmental pollution，逻辑并不复杂，按照谓语的顺序翻译即可。)

9. 土族塞浦路斯妇女在探索全岛统一并实现全民和平与繁荣的过程中起着非常重要的作用，特别是近15个月来土族塞浦路斯人的运动显示了这一点，该运动旨在支持和解并寻找解决塞浦路斯问题的联邦方案。(这句话的主结构是 The role of Turkish-Cypriot women also has been very important as regards the efforts for a solution that would reunify the island and lead to peace and prosperity for its entire people，这一部分放在译文的前面，中间的部分 as demonstrated in the emerging movement within the Turkish-Cypriot community in support of the efforts for reconciliation and the finding of a federal solution to the Cyprus problem, in particular in the last 15 months 可以放在后面。)

10. 未能严格履行本协议的条款、条件、约定等不应视为免除任何一方应有的权利或补偿，也不能视为免除协议、条款、约定后续违约行为或过错行为。(该句原文取自合同，主结构是 The failure to insist upon the strict performance of any of these agreements, terms, covenants or conditions hereof shall not be deemed a waiver of any rights or remedies or a waiver，waiver 后面跟了定语从句，这样分析以后翻译就不难了。)

第十九章　中文长句的翻译

中文属于意合语言，一句话要等意思都表达完整才使用句号，所以一般的中文句子均含有两个或两个以上的小分句。翻译中文长句时，一般说来，如果前后逻辑关系比较简单，能够找到一个分句作为英译文的主结构，其他部分可以变为次要结构，那么这个中文句子就可以译成一个英文句子。如果中文句子属于由若干个小句组成的流水句，两个或两个以上的部分都可以成为英语句子的主结构，这时要将句子按照意群和逻辑关系断句，把由不同主语组成的句子译成多个英文句子。

◇ 例1

火把节体现了彝族敬火、崇火的民族性格，保留着彝族起源发展的古老信息，是近距离体会彝族传统音乐、舞蹈、诗歌、饮食、服饰、天文等文化的绝佳机会。

这句话看起来比较长，但分析后会发现，句子的主结构是"火把节体现了彝族敬火、崇火的民族性格，保留着彝族起源发展的古老信息"，后面主要部分"是……机会"可以作为译文中的从属结构。当然，也可以把前面内容作为从属结构，后面内容作为主结构。这样分析以后，翻译就简单了。译文如下：

译文1：The Torch Festival embodies the Yi people's reverence of fire, and the Yi ethnic group's origin and development, providing an opportunity for visitors to experience the ethnic culture including music, dance, poetry, cuisine, costume and astronomy.

译文2：The Torch Festival, an embodiment of the Yi people's reverence of fire, and the Yi ethnic group's origin and development, provides an opportunity for visitors to experience the ethnic culture including music, dance, poetry, cuisine, costume and astronomy.

✧ 例 2

同时，按照"发展生产，保障供给"的总方针，这个组织发动和组织群众，禁鸦片，种粮食，兴水利，修道路，办工业，促商贸，保障军需民用，为根据地的巩固和发展，提供了坚强的物质保证。

阅读例2并对其进行分析会发现，这句话的主干是"这个组织发动和组织群众，禁鸦片，种粮食，兴水利，修道路，办工业，促商贸"，句首的"按照……的总方针"可以译为状语，句尾的"保障军需民用"和"为……提供了坚强的物质保证"这两个小分句实际上是目的，所以可以用不定式将这两个目的状语并列，也可以将"保障军需民用"用不定式来表示，后者用非限定性定语从句表示。

译文 1：Meanwhile, in accordance with the general policy of "developing production and ensuring supply", the department mobilized and organized the masses to ban opium, grow crops, build roads and water conservancy projects, set up industries, promote trades and commerce to secure both the military and civilian needs, which provided a strong material guarantee for the consolidation and development of the area.

译文 2：Meanwhile, in accordance with the general policy of "developing production and ensuring supply", the department mobilized and organized the masses to ban opium, grow crops, build roads and water conservancy projects, set up industries, promote trades and commerce to secure both the military and civilian needs, and thus to provide a strong material guarantee for the consolidation and development of the area.

✧ 例 3

在合作期间，如遇地震、台风、水灾、火灾、战争或其他不能预见的不可抗力事故，并且，其发生和后果不能防止和避免，从而直接影响合同的履行或者不能按约定的条件履行，遭遇上述不可抗力事故的一方，应立即将事故情况电报通知对方，并应在15天内提供事故的详细情况及由相关公正部门开具的有效证明文件，证明合同不能履行，或者部分不能履行，或者需要延期履行的理由。

例3出自合同文本，可以看作是一个条件复句，即前面假设一种情况，后面提出解决方案，考虑到英文合同文本中也常用较长的句子，所以应该译成一个英文句子。但每一部分细节内容很多，所以译文要注意在句内做适当调整。我们可以将整个句子进行如下切分和转换。

（1）条件句：在合作期间，如遇地震、台风、水灾、火灾、战争或其他不能预见的不可抗力事故，并且，其发生和后果不能防止和避免，从而直接影响合同的履行或者不能按约定的条件履行（Should either of the parties to the contract be prevented from executing the contract or executing it in accordance with the agreed conditions by force majeure, such as earthquakes, typhoon, flood, fire, war or other unforeseen events, whose occurrence and consequences are unpreventable and unavoidable）

（2）主结构：遭遇上述不可抗力事故的一方，应立即将事故情况电报通知对方，并应在15天内提供事故的详细情况及由相关公正部门开具的有效证明文件，证明合同不能履行，或者部分不能履行，或者需要延期履行的理由（the prevented party shall inform the other party thereof by telegram without delay, and within 15 days thereafter provide detailed information of the incident and a valid certificate as evidence thereof issued by competent notary authorities explaining the reason for its inability to execute or its delay in executing the contract or part of it）

例3译文如下：

Should either of the parties to the contract be prevented from executing the contract or executing it in accordance with the agreed conditions by force majeure, such as earthquakes, typhoon, flood, fire, war or other unforeseen events, and their occurrence and consequences are unpreventable and unavoidable, the prevented party shall notify the other party by telegram without delay, and within 15 days thereafter provide detailed information of the events and a valid document for evidence issued by the relevant public notary organization explaining the reason for its inability to execute or its delay in executing the contract or part of it.

同样，下面例句也出自法律文本，翻译时可以考虑译成一句话。前面是条件，后面是主结构。

◇ 例 4

股东会或者股东大会、董事会的会议召集程序、表决方式违反法律、行政法规或者公司章程，或者决议内容违反公司章程的，股东可以自决议作出之日起六十日内，请求人民法院撤销。

If the procedures for calling a shareholders' meeting or shareholders' assembly, or meeting of the board of directors, or the voting form, is in violation of any law, administrative regulation or the bylaw, or if a resolution is in violation of the bylaw of the company, the shareholders may, within 60 days from the day when the resolution is made, request the people's court to revoke it.

再来看几个中文长句。

◇ 例 5

人工智能时代，我们希望计算机拥有视觉、听觉、语言和行动的能力，其中语言是人类区别于动物的最重要特征之一，语言是人类思维的载体，也是知识凝练和传承的载体。

这句话经过分析可以发现，"人工智能时代，我们希望计算机拥有视觉、听觉、语言和行动的能力"和后面的"其中语言是人类区别于……也是知识凝练和传承的载体"关系并不密切。因此，翻译时要考虑将句子拆分。后面一部分都在描述语言，可以译成一个独立的英语句子，即主结构是"语言是特征和载体"。这样一来，整句话可以译为：

In an era of AI, the computer is expected to have the ability to see, hear, speak and act. Language is one of the most important characteristics that differentiate human beings from animals and the carrier of human thinking and of knowledge accumulated and passed-down by human beings.

◇ 例 6

陶瓷是中华五千年文明最为灿烂的文化符号之一，"china"在英文里原本的意思就是瓷器，能用它指代中国，主要是因为中国的瓷器在世界范围内受到极大的喜爱和推崇。

分析原文会发现，"陶瓷是中华五千年文明最为灿烂的文化符号之一"和后面"'china'在英文里原本的意思……受到极大的喜爱和推崇"关系并不紧密，所以考虑拆分句子。后面这一部分比较长，分析后发现可以将"'china'被用来指代中国"作为主结构，"主要是因为中国的瓷器……"可以作原因状语，"在英文里原本的意思就是瓷器"可以作china的定语。这样分析之后，就可以得到如下译文：

Porcelain is one of the most splendid cultural symbols of the Chinese civilization with a five-thousand-year history. The word "china", which originally means porcelain in English, is used to refer to the country, mainly because Chinese porcelain has been greatly favored and highly pursued worldwide.

◇ 例 7

景德镇瓷器之所以能闻名于世，主要是通过两个途径：一是明代航海家、外交家郑和（1371年—1433年）七次下西洋，其间他携带了大量的陶瓷制品和中国特产，而陶瓷作为承载着中国文明的载体，一进入欧洲便被贵族追捧，视为身份与地位的象征；二是陆上的丝绸之路，景德镇陶瓷兴盛之时，丝绸之路成为中外贸易的主要通道。大批的陶瓷制品，通过丝绸之路被销往外国。

经过分析发现，这句话有以下三层关系：

（1）景德镇瓷器之所以能闻名于世，主要是通过两个途径：Jingdezhen porcelain gained its notability in the world mainly in two ways.

（2）一是明代航海家、外交家郑和（1371年—1433年）七次下西洋，其间他携带了大量的陶瓷制品和中国特产，而陶瓷作为承载着中国文明的载体，一进入欧洲便被贵族追捧，视为身份与地位的象征：First, Zheng He (1371—1433), a navigator and diplomat in the Ming Dynasty, made seven voyages to the West, bringing there a large number of porcelain products and Chinese specialties.

As a carrier of Chinese civilization, porcelain was well-received by nobles as a symbol of identity and status upon its appearance in Europe.（这一部分依然很长，所以考虑拆分成两个句子。）

（3）二是陆上的丝绸之路，景德镇陶瓷兴盛之时，丝绸之路成为中外贸易的主要通道。大批的陶瓷制品，通过丝绸之路被销往外国：Second, the Silk Road on land became the main route for foreign trades when Jingdezhen porcelain flourished. A large number of porcelain products were sold to foreign countries via the Silk Road.（这一部分的后面与前面关系不十分密切，因此也考虑拆分。）

经过上面的分析，便可以得出以下译文：

Jingdezhen porcelain gained its notability in the world mainly in two ways. First, Zheng He (1371-1433), a navigator and diplomat in the Ming Dynasty, made seven voyages to the West, bringing there a large number of porceloin products and Chinese specialties. As a carrier of Chinese civilization, porcelain was well-received by nobles as a symbol of identity and status upon its appearance in Europe. Second, the Silk Road on land became the main route for foreign trades when Jingdezhen porcelain flourished. A large number of porcelain products were sold to foreign countries via the Silk Road.

通过以上中文长句的分析，我们不难发现，翻译汉语长句时，必须对原文的含义进行分析。若句中有多重含义，首先确定是否需要拆分，然后再分析每一句的主结构和次要结构是什么，再根据英语句子的特点和表达习惯将每一部分的内容再现出来，便可以得到完整而准确的译文。当然，要把握原文的逻辑关系，还要看译者的中英文基本功，因此，语言基本功训练不可忽视。

拓展练习

翻译下列句子，请注意中文长句的分析和翻译。

1. 这部电影让少林功夫成为当代武术最好、最高竞技的代名词，不仅在中国引导了一大波父母将自己的孩子送去河南的武校学武，在世界范围内，也吸引了大量的"洋学生"为中国武术痴狂。

2. 除此之外，清明节还可以植树、放风筝、荡秋千，江南地区还会举办蚕花会，有迎蚕神、摇快船、唱戏文等极具水乡特色的活动。

3. 14年后，人类面临着更加严峻的挑战和更为艰难的抉择，在各方努力下，北京冬奥会在世纪疫情中准时开幕，来自91个国家和地区的2892名运动员，以及更多教练员、技术人员、医疗团队成员和媒体记者等共同参加这场盛会。

4. 人们会在端午节这天手系五彩丝线，在家中悬挂艾草，举行拜神祭祖的仪式，品尝馅料繁多的粽子和美味的雄黄酒，在湖南汨罗每年还会举行热闹的赛龙舟活动，都是不容错过的体验。

5. 中国大力实施网络强国战略、国家信息化战略、国家大数据战略、"互联网+"行动计划，大力发展电子商务，着力推动互联网和实体经济深度融合发展，促进资源配置优化，促进全要素生产率提升，为推动创新发展、转变经济增长方式、调整经济结构发挥积极作用。

6. 《只有河南·戏剧幻城》是全世界规模最大、演出时长最长的戏剧聚落群，占地622亩，总投资金额60亿，这是一座有21个剧场、近千名演职人员的戏剧幻城，所有剧场可同时容纳一万名观众，所有剧目单次不重复演出总时长近700分钟。

7. 学院秉承"博识雅行，学游天下"的人才培养理念，培养具有宽广知识、完善人格、旅游情怀和国际视野，具有扎实的旅游专业知识和较强的实践能力，具有较强的社会责任感、创新创业精神和可持续发展能力的高素质应用型旅游人才。

8. 上海美术馆创建于1956年，是新中国最早建立的美术馆之一，拥有收藏美术精品、开展学术研究、举办陈列展览、普及审美教育、促进国际交流等多项功能，并与海内外著名美术馆建立合作关系。

9. 呼麦艺术历史悠久，早在12世纪蒙古高原的先民便在狩猎和游牧中虔诚模仿大自然的声音，他们认为，这是与自然、宇宙有效沟通、和谐相处的重要途径，由此人体发声器官的某些潜质得到开发，一人模仿瀑布、高山、森林、动物的声音时可以发出"和声"，这便是呼麦的雏形。

10. 公司股东应当遵守法律、行政法规和公司章程，依法行使股东权利，不得滥用股东权利损害公司或者其他股东的利益；不得滥用公司法人独立地位和股东有限责任损害公司债权人的利益。

参考译文与简析

1. The film made Shaolin *gongfu* the synonym of the best of martial arts and sports skills of the time. Then not only did many Chinese parents send their children to martial arts schools in Henan Province, but also many foreign students were fascinated by Chinese *gongfu*.（该句可以拆译为两个部分，第一部分是"这部电影让少林功夫成为当代武术最好、最高竞技的代名词"，第二部分用 not only...but also 连接，需要注意如果连接的是两个小分句，第一个小分句使用倒装。）

2. Moreover, the day is suited for planting trees, flying kites and playing on the swings. In southern China, the "Silkworm Flower Fair" will also take place, comprising events unique to water towns, including the welcoming of Silkworm God, boat racing and opera shows.（该句从意思上看，前面说的是整个清明节，后面说江南的清明节活动，因此也译成两个句子。另外，该句翻译还要注意将其中活动名称的翻译，既要简单，又要适当传达中国文化。）

3. Fourteen years later, the globe is confronted with more severe challenges and more difficult choices. Thanks to the efforts of all, the Beijing Winter Olympics opened on time despite the epidemic of the century. 2,892 athletes from 91 countries and regions, as well as coaches, technicians, medical workers and media reporters participated in this grand event.（原文的一句话翻译成了英文三句话。）

4. Some experiences should not be missed at the Duanwu Festival, for example, tying colorful silk threads on hands, hanging wormwood at home, holding ceremonies to worship deities and ancestors, eating *zongzi* with different stuffing, drinking palatable realgar wine, and enjoying the lively boat races held every year, especially on the Miluo River in Hunan.（原文主要写端午节的活动，所以可以先把主结构译出，即"人们在端午节不容错过一些体验"，然后举例即可。）

5. China is implementing the national strategies for cyber development, IT application, big data and the "Internet Plus" action plan. It encourages the development of e-commerce, promotes integration of the digital and real economies, optimizes the

allocation of resources and boosts total factor productivity, which will contribute to innovative development, economic growth mode transformation and economic structure adjustment.（这句话原文动词短语并列较多，但要分析其中的逻辑关系，可将"中国大力实施网络强国战略、国家信息化战略、国家大数据战略、'互联网+'行动计划"译为一句英语，然后再翻译"大力发展电子商务，着力推动互联网和实体经济深度融合发展，促进资源配置优化，促进全要素生产率提升"，最后的部分"为推动创新发展、转变经济增长方式、调整经济结构发挥积极作用"可以使用非限定性定语从句。）

6. Unique Henan—Land of Drama is the largest drama theater complex with the longest show hours in the world, covering an area of 102 acres, with a total investment of RMB 6 billion. It is a complex with 21 theaters and nearly 1,000 members of casting crew, and the theaters can accommodate an audience of 10,000, with the total length being nearly 700 minutes for a single round of non-repeating shows.（该句可以拆成两个句子翻译，第一句到"总投资金额60亿"，后面的"这是一座有21个剧场、近千名演职人员的戏剧幻城，所有剧场可同时容纳一万名观众，所有剧目单次不重复演出总时长近700分钟"译成了一个并列句。翻译中需要注意使用一些介词短语，如with短语使用了两次。）

7. The college adheres to the concept "Learn with Travel, Act with Grace", aiming to equip its students with multi-disciplinary knowledge, well-rounded personalities, tourism sentiment and international vision, so that they will be high-quality tourism talent with solid professional knowledge and capabilities, a strong sense of social responsibility, innovative entrepreneurship and sustainability awareness.（原文虽然比较长，但后面"人才"的修饰语多，因此译为一句话。）

8. Founded in 1956, Shanghai Art Museum is one of the earliest art museums in China, serving the purpose of arts collection, academic research, exhibition, aesthetic education and international communication. It has established partnership with arts museums of the world.（该句译成了两句英文，第一句较长，但使用了过去分词和现在分词短语。将"与……建立合作关系"另起一句。）

9. Khoomei has a long history. As early as the twelfth century, the Mongolian ancestors living on the Mongolian Plateau imitated the sound from nature when

they were hunting and herding. They regarded the imitation as an important way to communicate and get along harmoniously with nature and universe. Thus, some potential of the human vocal organs was developed, allowing one person to create "harmony" when he was imitating the sound of waterfalls, mountains, forests, and animals. That was the embryo of Khoomei. （该句介绍呼麦艺术，英语译文中句子不要过长，所以整个长句根据意群译成了五句英文。）

10. The shareholders of a company shall abide by the laws, administrative regulations and bylaw and shall exercise the shareholder's rights under the law. None of them may injure any of the interests of the company or of other shareholders by abusing the shareholder's rights, or injure the interests of any creditor of the company by abusing the independent status of legal person or the shareholder's limited liabilities. （该句取自合同文本，译文拆成了两句，第一句到"依法行使股东权利"，第二句较长。整个译文符合合同的文体特点。）

第二十章　英译中的合句处理

英文属于形合语言，在篇章中表现为形式完整的句子可以独立成句，不会考虑下一句的意思是否跟前面一句有关联。前一章提到，中文是意合语言，句子一般由多个意思相关的小分句组成。这说明，英文译成中文时，需要考虑译文是否符合中文的表达习惯，是否符合中文读者的预期。因此，英译中时，有时要考虑句与句之间的意思是否相关，如果相关，就要进行合句处理，即将意思相关的句子译成一个中文句子，即变为中文的小分句，中间用逗号分开，有时还要省译第二句的主语。特别是前后句子都比较短小的时候，更要考虑是否要合句翻译。

◇ 例1

In fact, most new managers see themselves as targets of organizational change initiatives, implementing with their groups the changes ordered from above. They don't see themselves as change agents.

这个例子中前一句可以翻译为"实际上，大多数新上任的管理者将自己视为公司变革行动的被动接受者，与自己的团队实施上级要求实施的改革"，后一句应该译为"他们不把自己视为改革的发起人。"这样看来，实际上两句话都在说"新上任的管理者"，因为后一句的they指代前一句主语most new managers。如果中文按照原文的标点符号进行翻译，译文如下。

译文1：实际上，大多数新上任的管理者将自己视为公司变革行动的被动接受者，与自己的团队实施上级要求实施的改革。他们不把自己视为改革的发起人。

这样的译文前后两句显得"格格不入"，中文读者会感觉句子有翻译腔。既然前后两句都在说"大多数新上任的管理者",不如将两部分合并,译成中文的小分句,后面的"他们"省译,甚至可以将后面较短的部分提到前面去。两种译文如下。

译文 2：实际上,大多数新上任的管理者将自己视为公司改革行动的被动接受者,与自己的团队实施上级要求实施的改革,而没有将自己视为改革的发起人。

或：实际上,大多数新上任的管理者没有将自己视为改革的发起人,而是公司改革行动的被动接受者,与自己的团队实施上级要求实施的改革。

对照译文 1 和译文 2,读者不难发现译文 2 的两种译法才是真正的中文,读起来自然流畅,没有生硬拗口的感觉。

◇ 例 2

Sustainability starts on a small scale, with each individual. We welcome projects by hotels that rely on heat pumps, wood heating, waste separation or waste heat and can thus offer climate-neutral holidays. Or by restaurants and shops that rely on regional products. Numerous hotels, restaurants, shops, mountain railways, other institutions and of course private individuals are setting a good example.

这个例子中 Or by restaurants and shops that rely on regional products 属于非主谓结构,单独成句是为了强调,意思与前面的 We welcome projects by hotels that rely on heat pumps, wood heating, waste separation or waste heat and can thus offer climate-neutral holidays 紧密相连。另外,从第二句开始实际上都是在进一步阐述第一句话,因此,中文不应该像下面这样拘泥于原文。

译文 1：可持续发展从小事做起,从我做起。我们欢迎酒店提供借助热泵、木材采暖、废物分离或废热实现气候中性的度假项目。也欢迎使用餐馆和商店本地产品。很多酒店、餐馆、商店、山区铁路以及其他机构和个人都树立了很好的榜样。

这个译文中间的句号会显得比较"扎眼",使得前后不太搭配,不如下面的译文更符合中文的习惯。

译文2：可持续发展从小事做起，从我做起。我们欢迎酒店提供借助热泵、木材采暖、废物分离或废热实现气候中性的度假项目，也欢迎使用餐馆和商店本地产品，而很多酒店、餐馆、商店、山区铁路以及其他机构和个人都树立了很好的榜样。

再来看更多的例子，不妨对译文1和译文2进行比较，你会发现哪种译文更符合中文的表达习惯。

◇ 例3

Fans of soft mobility, be it on foot or by bike, can choose among 2,500 miles of marked trails leading through varied and unusual scenery. Cogwheel trains allow you to reach the summits comfortably. They offer an incomparable view on the mountains and lakes.

译文1：对于"轻"出行爱好者而言，无论步行还是骑行，在2500英里的标记线路中，穿越各种各样独特风景，都能作出心仪的选择。齿轮铁路列车将您舒适地送达山顶。途中可以欣赏到无与伦比的群山和湖泊美景。

译文2：对于"轻"出行爱好者而言，无论步行还是骑行，在2500英里的标记线路中，穿越各种各样独特风景，都能作出心仪的选择。齿轮铁路列车将您舒适地送达山顶，途中可以欣赏到无与伦比的群山和湖泊美景。

◇ 例4

Ahead of the bleak and dark days of winter, trees reduce the chlorophyll in their leaves to safeguard all their valuable resources: the leaves send nitrogen, iron, manganese and other vital substances into the heart of the tree. These substances are then stored in the roots, branches and trunk until spring.

译文1：寒冷和黑暗的冬天来临之前，树木会减少叶子中的叶绿素，以保护自己宝贵的资源——叶子将氮、铁、锰和其他必要物质输送到树木中心。然后这些物质被储存在根、树枝和树干中一直到春天。

译文2：寒冷和黑暗的冬天来临之前，树木会减少叶子中的叶绿素，以保护自己宝贵的资源——叶子将氮、铁、锰和其他必要物质输送到树木中心，将这些物质储存在根、树枝和树干中，直至春天再次来临。

◇ 例 5

When a friend leaves for what was once a far country, even if he has no intention of returning, we cannot feel that same sense of irrevocable separation that saddened our forefathers. We know that he is only hours away by jet liner, and that we have merely to reach for the telephone to hear his voice.

译文 1：如果一位朋友启程前往曾被视为遥远的国家，即使他不打算回来，我们也无法像先辈一样，涌起因无法改变的分离而带来的悲伤。我们知道，这位朋友和我们之间只有喷气式飞机飞行几个小时的距离，我们只需拿起电话就能听到他的声音。

译文 2：如果一位朋友启程前往曾被视为遥远的国家，即使他不打算回来，我们也无法像先辈一样，涌起因无法改变的分离而带来的悲伤，因为我们知道，这位朋友和我们之间只有喷气式飞机飞行几个小时的距离，只需拿起电话就能听到他的声音。

◇ 例 6

The main goal of this climate protection programme is to supply poorer households and institutions such as schools in Uganda with new technologies to purify drinking water. The resulting reduced consumption of non-renewable firewood and charcoal reduces CO_2 emissions and at the same time has a positive impact on the living conditions and health of thousands of people.

译文 1：该气候保护计划主要旨在为乌干达贫困家庭和学校等机构提供净化饮用水的新技术。减少的不可再生木柴和木炭的消耗减少了二氧化碳排放，同时对成千上万人的生活条件和健康产生积极影响。

译文 2：该气候保护计划主要旨在为乌干达贫困家庭和学校等机构提供净化饮用水的新技术，以此减少不可再生木柴和木炭的消耗，从而减少二氧化碳排放，同时对成千上万人的生活条件和健康产生积极影响。

对比例 3 至例 6 的每两个译文，我们很容易发现，译文 2 均比译文 1 更通顺，更符合中文读者的预期，这是因为译文 2 根据中文的习惯对英文的两个句子进行了合句处理，而且使用了中文的小分句。这个技巧看似简单，大多数情况下只是一个小小的标点符号问题，但不少译者翻译时往往会拘泥原文的标点符号，使得译文显得比较拗口。因此，这一章就是提醒读者做翻译时要注意合句处理，使用中文小分句。

拓展练习

翻译下列篇章，请注意适当做合句处理。

1. This does not mean that the physical knowledge is already in hand for all problems of agriculture, energy, exploitation of water and mineral resources, pollution, or overpopulation. It does mean that man now has the tools to seek and find solutions to such problems and has already demonstrated in each category that solutions are possible.

2. First, two turbines were built. Within two years, the existing infrastructure for snowmaking was supplemented with elements for electricity production. This means that the investments already made in snowmaking can now also be used for the production of sustainable electricity. The overflow from captured drinking water sources enters the pipes. Then, as in any hydroelectric power plant, the water passes through the turbines and produces electrical energy. This is fed into the local power station and reaches the households in the surrounding area. Every year, the two power plants produce 800,000 kW·h of electricity. This corresponds to the annual consumption of about 200 households per year.

3. Zurich Tourism also highlights environmentally friendly tourist offers on its website with a green leaf. This allows guests to immediately recognize products and services that will not have a negative impact on the environment.

4. Switzerland's panorama train routes are among the most beautiful rail routes in the world. They pass through the most majestic mountain scenery, idyllic valleys and villages.

5. After tackling the subject of sustainability in depth at the organizational level, Zürich Tourism is now applying the same thinking at the level of the destination. It asked itself a fundamental question: Is it possible to market Zurich as a sustainable city?

6. First walk down the side street to the Tavel memorial. There are benches for you to sit and enjoy the view of Lake Thun, Niesen and Stockhorn. Then follow the sign for Bütschelegg. Once you reach the top of Bütschelegg, you can enjoy the wonderful autumn colours from the scenic overlook.

7. Cheeses from Switzerland are loved across the world. For its unique taste, its indisputable quality and its authenticity. Learn more about this famous, tasty, natural product.

8. Thanks to the innovative and efficient public transport system operating in Switzerland, international visitors can have their luggage transported by train direct to their holiday destination immediately after landing at either Zurich or Geneva Airport. There is no need to waste time waiting for their luggage.

9. The countries that the Nordic writers call home are prosperous and organised, a "soft society" according to Mr. Nesbo. But the protection offered by a cradle-to-grave welfare system hides a dark underside.

10. Four principal organs are located at the main UN Headquarters in New York City. The International Court of Justice is located in The Hague.

参考译文与简析

1. 这并不意味着人类掌握了有关农业、能源、水和矿产资源开发、污染或人口过剩等所有问题的全部自然科学知识，但这确实意味着，人类已经掌握了一定的工具用来寻求和找到这些问题的解决方案，并且各类别中均已证明可能存在解决方案。（原文是两句话，但两句在意思上是相连的，因此中文合并为一句，将两句之间的句号改为逗号。）

2. 首先，建造了两台涡轮机。两年内，现有造雪基础设施得到了电力生产设施的补充，这意味着已经在造雪方面进行的投资也可用于生产可持续电力。获取的溢流饮用水流入管道后，就像任何水力发电厂一样，水通过涡轮机产生电能，这些电能输送到当地电站，到达周边地区的千家万户。两座电厂每年发电量达 80 万千瓦时，相当于约 200 户家庭每年的电力消费。(Within two years, the existing infrastructure for snowmaking was supplemented with elements for electricity production 和 This means that the investments already made in snowmaking can now also be used for the production of sustainable electricity 意思相连，因此译文将中间的句号改为逗号。The overflow from captured drinking water sources enters the pipes、Then, as in any hydroelectric power plant, the water passes through the turbines and produces electrical energy 和 This is fed into the local power station and reaches the households in the surrounding area 三句话在意思上是相连的，因此作合句处理。)

3. 苏黎世旅游局还在其网站上用绿叶标志突出了环保旅游的优惠，帮助游客立即识别出不会对环境产生负面影响的产品和服务。(后一句中的 this 指前面提及的内容，因此意思相连，翻译时合句。)

4. 瑞士的全景观列车线路堪称全世界最美丽的铁路线路之一，穿过最壮丽的高山美景和如诗如画的山谷和村庄。(第二句的主语 they 指第一句的主语 Switzerland's panorama train routes，意思是相连的，因此作合句处理。)

5. 在组织层面深入解决可持续发展问题后，苏黎世旅游局现在正在旅游目的地层面应用落实同样的想法，同时也向自身提出了一个基本问题：是否有可能将苏黎世作为一座可持续发展的城市进行推广？(后一句中的 it 指前一句的主语 Zurich Tourism，所以可以合句，译为中文连动式。)

6. 首先，沿着小巷来到塔维尔纪念碑，这里有长椅供游客坐下来欣赏图恩湖、尼森和施托克峰的景色，然后沿着 Bütschelegg 的路标前行，到达 Bütschelegg 山顶后，可以在风景优美的观景台欣赏美妙的秋色。(原句取自旅游素材，每一句话都比较短，但实际上连贯性很强，因此翻译时作合句处理。)

7. 来自瑞士的奶酪深受世界各地的人们喜爱，因为瑞士奶酪风味独特，使用真材实料，品质无可置疑。欢迎深入了解这种著名的天然美味产品。(原文前两句意思关联，因此翻译时作了合句处理。)

8. 借助瑞士富有创意的高效公共交通运输网络，国际游客可在抵达苏黎世机场或日内瓦机场后马上将自己的行李通过火车直接运往自己的度假目的地，无须浪费时间等待领取行李。(虽然原文第一句较长，第二句较短，但第二句在意思上与第一句关联，因此翻译时作了合句处理。）

9. 北欧作家称之为家的国家都繁荣而且秩序井然，是奈斯博所谓的"软社会"，但是终生福利制度提供的保障掩盖了黑暗的一面。（原文第二句和第一句有一定的转折关系，意思相连，因此可以合句。）

10. 联合国四大主要机构设于纽约市联合国总部，国际法院设于荷兰海牙。（很明显，两句意思密切，因此翻译时合句处理。）

主要参考文献

［1］ Catford, J.C. A Linguistic Theory of Translation［M］. London: Oxford University Press, 1965.

［2］ Halliday, M. A. K. & R. Hasan. Cohesion in English［M］. London and New York: Longman, 1976.

［3］ Leo Tolstoy. Russia's Thunderous Prophet［J］. 英语文摘，2011（2）：49—52.

［4］ Newmark, P. A Textbook of Translation［M］. Shanghai: Shanghai Foreign Language Education Press, 2001.

［5］ Newmark, P. Approaches to Translation［M］. UK: Prentice Hall International Ltd., 1988.

［6］ Nida, E. & C. Taber. The Theory and Practice of Translation［M］. Leiden: Brill, 1969.

［7］ Nida, E.A. Language and Culture—Contexts in Translating［M］. Shanghai: Shanghai Foreign Language Education Press, 2001.

［8］ Pinham, J. The Translator's Guide to Chinglish（中式英语之鉴）［M］. Beijing: Foreign Language Teaching and Research Press，2000.

［9］ Quirk, R.& S. Greenbaum. et. al. A Grammar of Contemporary English［M］. UK: Longman Group UK Limited, 1973.

［10］ Thackeray, W. M. *Vanity Fair*［M］. UK：Wordsworth Editions Limited, 1993.

［11］ Mitchell, M. Gone with the Wind［M］. Beijing: China Aerospace Publishing House, 2011.

［12］ 陈德彰. 英汉翻译入门［M］. 北京：外语教学与研究出版社，2005.

［13］ 陈世彬. 金融翻译技法［M］. 北京：中国对外翻译出版公司，2002.

［14］顾维勇.实用文体翻译［M］.北京：国防工业出版社，2005.

［15］连淑能.英汉对比研究［M］.北京：高等教育出版社，1992.

［16］刘宓庆.翻译教学：实务与理论［M］.北京：中国对外翻译出版公司，2003.

［17］刘宓庆.翻译与语言哲学［M］.北京：中国对外翻译出版公司，2001.

［18］吕叔湘.中国人学英语［M］.北京：中国社会科学出版社，2005.

［19］彭萍.实用旅游英语翻译（英汉双向）［M］.北京：对外经济贸易大学出版社，2016.

［20］彭萍.实用商务翻译（英汉双向）［M］.北京：中国宇航出版社，2015.

［21］彭萍.实用英汉对比与翻译（英汉双向）［M］.北京：中译出版社，2015.

［22］彭萍.实用语篇翻译（英汉双向）［M］.北京：中国宇航出版社，2015.

［23］彭萍.新编商务英语翻译教程［M］.北京：商务印书馆，2021.

［24］彭萍.英汉笔译［M］.北京：外语教学与研究出版社，2017.

［25］乔萍等.散文佳作108篇［Z］.北京：外文出版社，2004.

［26］邵志洪.汉英对比翻译导论［M］.上海：华东理工大学出版社，2005.

［27］史密斯.二十世纪视觉艺术.［M］.彭萍译.北京：中国人民大学出版社，2007.

［28］许建平.英汉互译实践与技巧［M］.北京：清华大学出版社，2008.

［29］杨自伍.英国散文名篇欣赏［Z］.上海：上海外语教育出版社，1995.

［30］詹姆斯等.旋转的螺丝钉［M］.刘勃，彭萍译.北京：中国人民大学出版社，2004.

［31］张法连.法律英语翻译教程［M］.北京：北京大学出版社，2016.

［32］张培基.英汉翻译教程［M］.上海：上海外语教育出版社，1983.